MULTIPROCESSOR PERFORMANCE

WILEY SERIES IN PARALLEL COMPUTING

SERIES EDITORS:

J.W. de Bakker, *Centrum voor Wiskunde en Informatica, The Netherlands*
M. Hennessy, *University of Sussex, UK*
D. Simpson, *Brighton Polytechnic, UK*

Carey (ed.): Parallel Supercomputing: Methods, Algorithms and Applications

de Bakker (ed.): Languages for Parallel Architectures: Design, Semantics, Implementation Models

Axford: Concurrent Programming: Fundamental Techniques for Real-Time and Parallel Software Design

Gelenbe: Multiprocessor Performance

Treleaven (ed.): Parallel Computers: Object-oriented, Functional and Logic

MULTIPROCESSOR PERFORMANCE

Erol Gelenbe

Université René Descartes, France

JOHN WILEY & SONS
Chichester · New York · Brisbane · Toronto · Singapore

Copyright © 1989 by John Wiley & Sons Ltd.
Baffins Lane, Chichester
West Sussex PO19 1UD, England

All rights reserved.

No part of this book may be reproduced by any means, or transmitted, or translated into a machine language without the written permission of the publisher.

Other Wiley Editorial Offices

John Wiley & Sons, Inc., 605 Third Avenue,
New York, NY 10158-0012, USA

Jacaranda Wiley Ltd, G.P.O. Box 859, Brisbane,
Queensland 4001, Australia

John Wiley & Sons (Canada) Ltd, 22 Worcester Road,
Rexdale, Ontario M9W 1L1, Canada

John Wiley & Sons (SEA) Pte Ltd, 37 Jalan Pemimpin   05-04,
Block B, Union Industrial Building, Singapore 2057

Library of Congress Cataloging-in-Publication Data:

Gelenbe, E., 1945 –
 Multiprocessor performance / Erol Gelenbe
   p. cm. – (Wiley series in parallel computing)
 Includes bibliographical references.
 ISBN 0 471 92392 3
 1. Multiprocessors—Evaluation. I. Title. II. Series.
QA76.9.E94G45   1989
004'.355 – dc20   89-36431
                                                                 CIP

British Library Cataloguing in Publication Data:

Gelenbe, E. (Erol), *1945 –*
 Multiprocessor performance. – (Wiley series in
 parallel computing).
  1. Computer systems. Multiprocessors
004'.35
ISBN 0 471 92392 3

Printed in Great Britain by Courier International, Tiptree, Essex

à mes parents

Contents

1 **Introduction to Multiprocessor Performance**   1
    1.1 Introduction 1
    1.2 Contents of the Monograph 3
    1.3 Acknowledgements 5

2 **Multiprocessor Architecture, Program Structure, and Machine Performance**   7
    2.1 Introduction 7
    2.2 Performance Potential and Limitations of Parallel Computer Architectures 10
    2.3 Performance Issues in some Typical Multiprocessor Architectures 12
    2.4 Different Types of Multiprocessors 15
    2.5 Conclusions 19
    2.6 Bibliography 19

3 **Multiprocessor Speed-up and Amdahl's Law**   21
    3.1 Introduction 21
    3.2 An Amendment to Amdahl's Law 23
       3.2.1 The Most Favourable Case 23
       3.2.2 The Least Favourable Case 24
       3.2.3 Amendment to Amdahl's Law when Communication is Neglected 24
       3.2.4 The effect of Communication Time between Parallel Processors 24
    3.3 A Model of Intrinsic Program Behaviour 25
       3.3.1 A Statistical Interpretation 28
       3.3.2 A Numerical Example 28
    3.4 Conclusions 29

	3.5	Bibliography	30

4 Performance of Interconnection Networks — 33

- 4.1 Introduction — 33
- 4.2 Bandwidth of the Baseline and Omega Networks with the Drop Approach — 36
- 4.3 Numerical Solution of the DROP Model — 40
- 4.4 Bandwidth of the DROP Model — 41
- 4.5 The HOLD Network Model — 42
- 4.6 Bibliography — 46

5 Parallel Program Performance: Series-Parallel Program Structures — 49

- 5.1 Introduction — 49
- 5.2 The SPTG Model of Program Structure — 50
  - 5.2.1 Stochastic Model for a Family of SPTG — 52
  - 5.2.2 Statistical Properties of the Family of SPTG — 55
- 5.3 Distribution of Program Execution or Completion Time — 58
- 5.4 Numerical Solution for the Execution Time Distribution Function — 60
  - 5.4.1 The Computational Algorithm — 62
  - 5.4.2 A Numerical Example — 62
- 5.5 Bibliography — 64

6 General Acyclic Random Graphs as Models of Parallel Programs — 67

- 6.1 Introduction — 67
  - 6.1.1 A random graph model for a family of programs — 72
- 6.2 Asymptotic Properties of the Speed-up — 75
- 6.3 Asymptotic Analysis of the Mean Processing Time — 76
- 6.4 Comparison of the Approximation with Simulation Results — 78
- 6.5 Estimation of p the Probability of Precedence between Tasks — 79
  - 6.5.1 Estimating p from the Indegree of a Randomly Chosen Node — 80
  - 6.5.2 Estimating p from the Number of Roots of the Task Graph — 82

	6.5.3	Estimating p from the Number of Edges in the Graph 83
6.6		Task Graphs with Communication Times between Tasks 83
	6.6.1	Asymptotic properties of task graphs with communication times 86
	6.6.2	A simulation example of asymptotic speed-up with communication times 88
6.7		Bibliography 90

7 Multiprocessor Performance with Task-Graph Models   93
- 7.1 Introduction 93
- 7.2 The Multiprocessor System Model 94
  - 7.2.1 The General System Model 95
  - 7.2.2 The Simplified Model 96
- 7.3 Derivation of the Job Response Time 98
- 7.4 Numerical Examples and Model Validation 103
- 7.5 Extension of the Method to the Analysis of Multiprocessor Systems with Different Types of Parallel Programs 107
- 7.6 The Case of Systems with Processors of Different Types 109
  - 7.6.1 Application of the Method to a System with Series-Parallel Task Graphs 115
- 7.7 Bibliography 117

8 Supercomputer Performance Evaluation   121
- 8.1 Introduction 121
- 8.2 Performance of a Single Processor 123
- 8.3 Supercomputers with Multiple Vector Processors 125
- 8.4 Supercomputers with a Limited Number of Vector Processing Facilities 128
  - 8.4.1 N_v vector processors and an unlimited number of scalar processors 129
  - 8.4.2 N_v vector processors and a single scalar processor ... 130
  - 8.4.3 The improvement resulting from the use of a larger number of processors 130
- 8.5 Los Alamos Benchmark Characteristics 132
- 8.6 Bibliography 134

9 Performance Analysis of the Connection Machine — 137
- 9.1 Introduction — 137
- 9.2 ROUTER Network Performance — 141
- 9.3 Highly Balanced Computations — 146
  - 9.3.1 The lightly loaded ROUTER network — 148
  - 9.3.2 A simple concrete example — 151
- 9.4 Conclusions — 151
- 9.4 Bibliography — 152

Index — 155

1

Introduction to Multiprocessor Performance

1.1 Introduction

Computer systems which are based on architectures composed of multiple processors have been with us for a long time. Indeed, they have been commonly available since the early 1970's with third generation architectures in which an input−output processor has accompanied the central processing unit, discharging it of tasks associated with transfers to secondary memory and input−output devices. This common form of parallelism has given rise to many of the interesting operating system synchronization problems which have been dealt with in the literature, and has lead to notable improvements in system performance. Not least of the consequences of this simple multiprocessing has been the introduction of virtual memory systems which would have been practically impossible if input−output processors (or channels, as they are sometimes called) had not existed.

Traditionally, high performance computer systems have used vector and array processors in order to increase the number of instructions executed per unit time. Furthermore, the vector or array processors themselves have used pipelining rather than parallelism. Multiprocessor architectures, going beyond the usual parallelism between input−output and central processing of instructions, have appeared initially, and rather timidly, in systems where redundancy was used in order to achieve a higher degree of availability and reconfigurability in case of failures.

On the other hand, distributed system architectures started appearing in the 1980's outside the research laboratory environment with the proliferation of personal workstations, personal computers and local area networks. In the area of telecommunications, multiprocessor architectures were also introduced at a rather early stage as a means to achieve higher availability and reconfigurability, and higher performance in a distributed environment.

Thus high performance multiprocessing systems are a relatively recent 'arrival' in the computer field. Their presence is inevitable however, and we may expect that the very high performance machines of the future will combine distributed computation, with array processing and with multiprocessing so as to make the best use of all available approaches.

Indeed, it is intuitively obvious that one can build machines with very high raw processing power using relatively conventional technology if a very large number of microprocessors or other types of logical or arithmetic processors can be connected together in the same machine. It is then necessary to have a sophisticated communication medium and architecture, such as an interconnection network, if the exchange of information between processors and between processors and memory is not to become a major bottlenecks and source of slowdown.

If the same application program is going to take advantage of a large number of processors, not only must it have the potential to do so as far as the application it is running is concerned, but some difficult programming and interprocess communication problems will also have to be solved.

Multiprocessors are the only direction one can take in the hope for unlimited processing power. We know that the intrinsic speed of electronic components is limited by physical considerations, including distances (which cannot be smaller than certain physically feasible lengths), component sizes (each component must contain a sufficiently large number of atoms if it is not going to be a 'random' object), and the speed of holes and electrons or photons in the physical medium. Thus we can only increase processing power indefinitely if we increase the degree of parallelism. This may be achieved to a certain extent by increasing the size of words in the computer, or by increasing the number of simultaneously active processors. Instruction speed can also be increased by simplifying the set of instructions used, as in reduced instruction set architectures. Ultimately, multiprocessors alone offer 'unlimited' speed-up.

As mentioned above, none of these classes is 'closed'; many real systems incorporate properties of more than one class. For instance the Hypercube architecture can be viewed both as a multiprocessor and as a distributed system. The class of multiprocessor architectures will itself incorporate a

1. Introduction

wide variety of machines.

The purpose of the present monograph is to address the major performance issues related to increasing computer performance via multiprocessing, with emphasis on program behaviour and performance modelling.

1.2 Contents of the Monograph

This monograph is organized in relatively self-contained chapters, each of which covers a major aspect of multiprocessor performance. Only chapters 5 and 6 are an exception to this rule since they both deal with graph representations of parallel programs.

In Chapter 2 we introduce and discuss various aspects of what one may call 'parallel' architectures, including vector or array processors, distributed systems, and multiprocessor systems. We compare these three large classes of architectures in general terms on the basis of speed, cost, reliability and other measures. We discuss the role of the architecture and of the operating system in a parallel architecture. We also survey broad classes of multiprocessor architectures, including conventional multiprocessors, hypercubes, the Connection Machine, and Lattice Gas machines, after showing that multiprocessors present the greatest potential for performance increase. Chapter 2 constitutes the real introduction to the rest of this book.

In Chapter 3 we begin the discussion of the effect of program behaviour on multiprocessor performance. We recall the earliest model used, known as Amdahl's Law, which relates the number of processors to the speed-up which may be expected. We introduce refinements and extensions to Amdahl's Law which include the effect of load imbalance as well as communication times between tasks in a parallel program. We then introduce a natural model of parallel program behaviour, called the Activity Set Model, which allows us to deduce bounds on the speed-up from knowledge of the intrinsic behaviour of a parallel program.

In Chapter 4 we turn our attention to interconnection networks. Indeed, one may consider that they are the key, as far as machine architecture is concerned, to the construction of very large multiprocessors. Their performance is therefore a crucial issue. Performance evaluation and prediction of interconnection networks, which are designed to provide non-blocking instruction and data transfer between memories and processors, is particularly difficult for several reasons. On the one hand, they are very large (in general they will contain of the order of N.log N elements for the connection of N processors to the same number of memory modules). Furthermore all of their elements are interconnected and therefore coupled. Also, the events for which these networks have to be evaluated, such as blocking or interference between different communication circuits or data packets, are supposed to be rare so that measurement and simulation become a delicate issue. In this chapter we present a modelling method which combines detailed representation of a communication path, with approximate representation of the interaction between paths much as is done in some very large physics models, in order to obtain an accurate performance model of such systems.

The approach to program behaviour modelling taken in Chapter 3 is quite global in that the internal behaviour of program execution is not represented but merely 'observed'. In Chapter 5 and 6 we enter into a detailed representation of the execution sequence of a parallel program. A task graph model is introduced in order to represent the intertask precedence relations within a program, the task execution times, as well as the times necessary to transfer data or other information from one task to the other during execution. In Chapter 5 we examine parallel programs whose execution sequence has a series-parallel structure, and develop a methodology to predict the best speed-up which can be obtained with such programs, as well as to obtain estimates of the number of processors that they actually will need to execute in the fastest possible manner. In Chapter 6 we consider task graphs with an arbitrary structure, for which we show that the best possible execution time will increase linearly with the number of individual executable tasks which are contained in the program. Under restrictive assumptions we also compute the approximate value of the proportionality constant, and present simulations for parameter values which are not covered by the theory. The use of such estimates for the judicious allocation of an appropriate number of processors to the execution of a parallel program is also suggested.

Chapter 7 is devoted to evaluating the performance of a multiprocessor system to which parallel programs arrive in the form of task graphs. An approximate analytical method based on queueing networks is developed, and simulations are presented for a variety of task graphs.

The need for very high performance computing in certain numerical applications and the performance of potential of supercomputers is discussed in Chapter 8. A simple analytical methodology is suggested, and then used to predict the effect of introducing multiple vector and scalar processors in a supercomputer architecture. Data from the well known Los Alamos benchmark is then used to obtain quantitative performance predictions and evaluations.

1. Introduction

Finally, in Chapter 9 we deal with the Connection Machine (trademark of the Thinking Machines Corporation) which designates a novel multiprocessor architecture containing several thousand very elementary processors, interconnected by a two level network architecture. The influence of the communication network on the machine's performance is discussed. An important aspect which is taken into consideration is the locality of the communication patterns between processors during program execution.

Each chapter is accompanied by a bibliography intended both for background and for further reading.

1.3 Acknowledgements

This monograph is based on research which the author undertook at the ISEM Laboratory of Université Paris-Sud (Orsay) between 1984 and 1987, and then at Ecole des Hautes Etudes en Informatique (EHEI), Université de Paris V.

Throughout the years, the continuing support of C3-CNRS (French National Program in Parallel and Distributed Computing) and of its Distributed Algorithms Section has been very valuable.

CNET (Centre National d'Etudes des Telecommunications), has supported some of the modelling work described in this book. The French electronics and telecommunications company SAGEM SA has funded some of its applications to their multiprocessor systems; the author thanks Pierre Faurre and Michel Métivier for their trust.

A number of former graduate students, including François Baccelli, Guy Bernard, Jean-Michel Fourneau, Geneviève Jomier, Brigitte Plateau, and Catherine Rosenberg have been a source of encouragement and friendly support.

The pleasant atmosphere created by Norbert Cot, Dominique Fortier and Georges Stamon at EHEI is gratefully acknowledged.

Some of the work presented in this monograph was carried out at institutions which the author visited, including the IBM Research Centres at Yorktown Heights and Zurich, and RIACS at the NASA Ames Research Centre, as well as the Computer Science Department at Stanford University. Most of the writing was carried out while the author was visiting the Management Science Group at Columbia University's Graduate School of Business in the Fall of 1988.

Joint work related to multiprocessor performance was done with several colleagues, including Randy Nelson and Asser Tantawi of Yorktown Heights, and with former graduate students Euripides Montagne, Rina Suros and Zhen Liu. Discussions with Nihal Pekergin, Sophie Lefebvre and Jean-Marc Vincent are also gratefully acknowledged.

The preparation of the camera ready copy for this book was carried out with great diligence and patience by Marisela Hernández and Nihal Pekergin.

The author is also grateful to his editor at John Wiley & Sons, Gaynor Redvers-Mutton, for her very cooperative attitude, and to Stuart Gale, the Senior Desk Editor, for his careful review of an initial version of the manuscript.

2

Multiprocessor Architecture, Program Structure, and Machine Performance

2.1 Introduction

The appeal of computer architectures with multiple processors, which we consider in this chapter in the widest possible sense, lies in the hope for ever-increasing performance. Ideally, the performance of a multiprocessor architecture should increase linearly with the number of processors in the system. This may be true for certain applications which are then said to be 'scalable' [1] for some type of architecture. In many cases, however, this will not be true for a number of reasons.

In this chapter we shall present a panorama of the issues which influence performance for different types of 'parallel' architectures.

The relationship between a potentially parallel application and the architectures which may take advantage of this parallelism is shown schematically below:

Potentially Parallel Application (PPA)	⟶	Parallel System Architecture (PSA)	⟶	Parallel Computer Architecture (PCA)

We shall say that an application program is a PPA if it can be structured and programmed in the form of a set of *cooperating sequential processes* which may

- *share* resources (for instance memory),
- *exchange* information (by message passing or by access to common data),
- possibly *call* or *activate* each other.

A PPA will have to be written in a programming language where the nature of these cooperating sequential processes becomes explicit, and then processed by an adequate compiler or interpreter, before parallelism can be usefully exercised.

Often one talks about the *granularity* of a PPA. This concept is related to the 'size' of each sequential process, expressed in terms of the number of instructions or the execution time. The granularity of a PPA is said to be coarse if the sequential processes it contains are large, and it is said to be fine (or fine-grained) if the sequential processes contain a small number of instructions to be executed.

The PSA handles the system functions which make parallelism meaningful. This includes allocating processors to sequential processes, organizing resource sharing and the exchange of information or messages among sequential processes, handling mutual calls between processes, etc. It will also organize the allocation of the resources of the PCA to one or more PPAs. More generally, its role is to recognize the parallelism (or lack of parallelism) in the code generated for the PPA, and organize its execution on the PCA. This will obviously depend strongly on the PCA's structure. Parallel Computer Architectures (PCA) may be very broadly put into four classes. Many practical systems in fact combine characteristics of each of these classes, which are the following.

- *Array processors*: are parallel computer architectures which deal primarily with repetitive and time synchronous operations on 'low level' data objects, with fine granularity. They are typically used for numerical computation and in applications in which the structure of the data objects is well known in advance (e.g. vectors or matrices). Array processors are an example of SIMD (single instruction multiple data) architectures. Typically, communication between sequential processes in this case will be achieved by sharing a *common memory*. Due to the fine level of granularity and the synchronism of its operations, an

2.1. Introduction

array processor will rely heavily on the speed and efficiency of the bus or *interconnection network* which carries the data between the memory and processors.

- *Distributed architectures*: are composed of relatively *autonomous subsystems* which are capable of handling complete system and execution functions, and which cooperate together to run a large application. Typical PPAs which are run on distributed architectures are distributed databases, distributed operating systems, etc. We are dealing here with *coarse-grained parallelism*. Communication within a distributed system is usually handled by a local area network, and the sequential processes running on the system will usually communicate by message passing or by remote procedure calls. Such architectures are becoming very common since they can be conveniently extended to meet needs for increasing computing capacity and services, as in the case of networks of workstations and file servers. One can also expect that some very large and apparently centralized computer system will in fact be structured in this manner.

- *Multiprocessors*: are architectures composed of multiple computing units which operate in asynchronous mode. Both fine-grained and coarse-grained parallelism can be achieved with multiprocessor architectures, although the former is more common. Generally, both local and shared memory can be available for the processors, and communication is achieved via a high speed bus or interconnection network. It is more common to deal with multiprocessors in which sequential processes communicate via access to shared memory, though message passing is sometimes used.

- *Data flow architectures*: are functionally distributed architectures using fine-grained parallelism. Here sequential processes or sets of instructions are associated with certain processors, and computations are triggered by the arrival of data at these processors. Individual or structured data objects therefore control the sequence of program execution in such systems. Their effectiveness will therefore depend largely on the speed and efficiency of the communication system being used, as well as on the manner in which the sequential processes have been chosen and allocated to the processors. They may be viewed as very general MIMD (multiple instruction multiple data) parallel architectures.

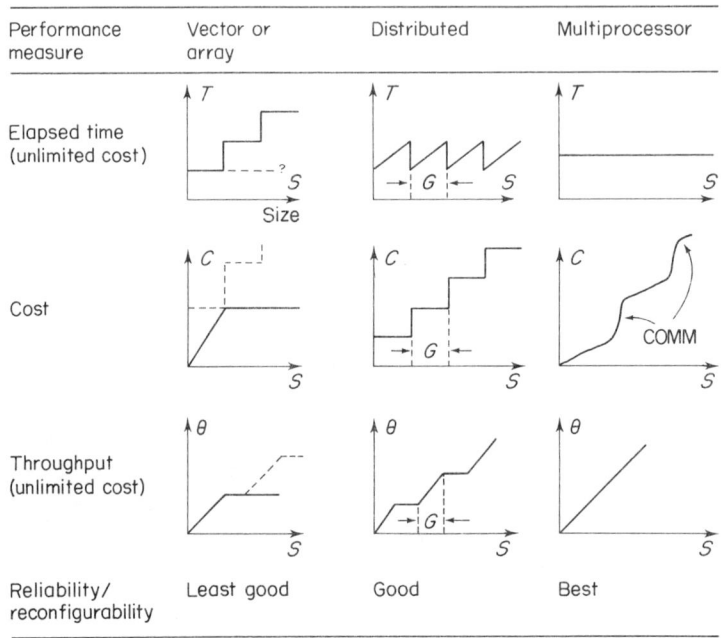

Figure 2.1: Simplified performance potential of the three major classes of parallel computer architectures

As mentioned above, none of these four classes is 'closed', in the sense that many real systems incorporate properties of more than one class. For instance the Hypercube architecture [2] which will be discussed below can be viewed both as a multiprocessor and as a distributed system. The class of multiprocessor architectures will itself incorporate a wide variety of machines, some of which will be discussed below.

2.2 Performance Potential and Limitations of Parallel Computer Architectures

The performance potential and limitations of the three most common PCAs is summarized on Fig. 2.1, which must be interpreted as a very simplified and qualitative presentation of performance characteristics rather than as a quantitatively significant indication.

Here we have compared Array, Distributed and Multiprocessor architectures with respect to four measures of interest: Elapsed Time (T) for

2.2. Performance Potential and Limitations ...   11

an application, Cost of the architecture (C), Throughput (θ), and Reliability/Reconfigurability. In each case (except for the last 'measure'), the abscissa of the curves is the *size* S of the application, in number of instructions and amount of data.

T is the time it takes to run the application assuming we are willing to make an unlimited investment (or amount of money) in the architecture we choose. We do assume, however, that all three classes of architectures are built with whatever technology is available at some given time. Thus as the size of the application increases, we allow ourselves to assume that (due to our unlimited cost constraint) we can purchase a larger configuration of each of the three types.

We show T increasing in steps as S increases for an *array processor*. This is because, even though S increases, the number and size of the arrays which the problem contains will be constrained by the physical problem which the application is solving. Thus an array processor will ultimately handle arrays whose size is determined by the application and not by the size of the array processor. Of course, we may be able to use several array processors simultaneously, but we are then combining array processors within a multiprocessor.

For a *multiprocessor*, which relies on increasing the number of processors as S (the problem size) increases, we can hope for a nearly flat curve for T since additional work will be done in parallel. Of course this is a simplification, as the more detailed discussion of subsequent chapters will show.

A *distributed* architecture should be quite comparable to a multiprocessor with respect to T, except for the granularity G. Indeed the T versus S characteristic for a multiprocessor will be obtained when G is very small. Unfortunately it is known that the practical performance of distributed systems is severely reduced if the operating system functions are distributed, so that the indications given here are optimistic lower bounds to what one might actually observe.

If one considers now the manner in which the cost C varies as the problem size S increases, assuming that the objective is to maximize performance, one can turn to the second set of curves of Fig. 2.1. The size of an array processor need not increase as the problem size increases; at some point its size will suffice to handle all the arrays which may be encountered in practice, hence its cost will remain constant as a function of problem size. The size of a distributed system and hence its cost will follow, in steps related to the granularity G, the size of the problem and the cost of the distributed system will follow suit. The size of a multiprocessor system, in terms of the number of processors and the size of memory, will also increase in proportion to S; however the cost will increase as shown in the figure due to the cost of the communication system. Indeed, when the size of the architecture passes a certain value the communication system (COMM) has to be replaced by a more sophisticated and hence more expensive system. We therefore have linear increases in cost for a given communication system as the size of application (and therefore of the system) increases, and then we have very rapid cost increases in cost due to the need for a new communication system.

The throughput curves, with unlimited cost, are easy to understand; here θ can be considered to be the number of instructions executed per unit time.

All these curves, and in particular the ones related to multiprocessor architectures, assume that the intrinsic parallelism within the code has some constant value which allows us to keep busy a number of processors which is proportional to the total number of processors available. We shall examine this aspect in great detail in later chapters.

Another important measure is the system reliability. A multiprocessor system may be constructed by duplicating subsystems so that each component subsystem can duplicate other subsystems as is done in standby redundant computer systems. Thus one can achieve as high a level of reliability as one may wish with a multiprocessor system, as is done currently in telephone switching computers, as long as cost is not an issue. Distributed architectures are also amenable to reliability improvements of the same sort though they need special concurrency control algorithms which take into account system reconfigurations in case of failures. Array architecture are essentially fully centralized systems; therefore they offer no particular reliability improvement with respect to conventional centralized machines.

We thus see that multiprocessor architectures offer the greatest potential for performance. We shall therefore examine in greater detail a certain number of architectures of this type.

2.3 Performance Issues in some Typical Multiprocessor Architectures

Two versions of a typical multiprocessor architecture are shown in Fig. 2.2.

The architecture considered contains p processors and m main memory banks organized around a bus, which could also be an interconnection network or a switch. Any processor can communicate with any main memory

2.3. Performance Issues in some Typical ...

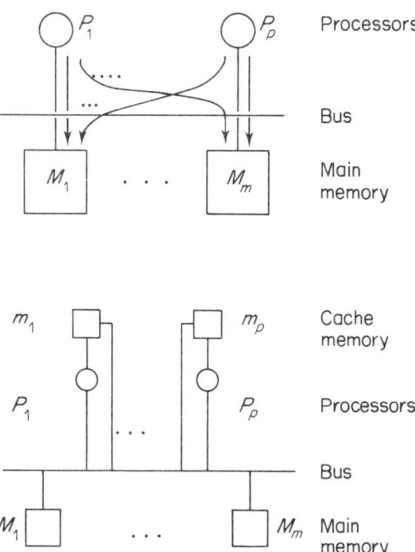

Figure 2.2: Two versions (with and without cache memories) of a typical multiprocessor architecture

bank. In the version with cache memories, these are private memory areas for the processors. Performance limitations of such systems arise from several factors including the following:

- The *bus* which carries instructions and data between the processors and the main memory; bus saturation will limit throughput. Thus high performance systems will require that it be replaced by a more sophisticated switch or interconnection network. Cache memories can alleviate some of this effect.

- The *main memory* is organized in memory banks so as to interleave access from the processors and thus reduce the probability of conflict between processors which may need to access the same memory bank. Furthermore, page faults in main memory will very obviously slow down considerably the system.

- The *cache memory* is a local memory for each of the processors which allows each processor a greater latitude with respect to accesses to main memory. It therefore accelerates the processor cycles, and reduces delays at the bus and at the main memory. As a consequence precautions have to be taken so as to maintain consistency of the data in cache with respect to main memory contents. One approach taken is to carry out write operations simultaneously in both memories; another is to copy portions of the cache back into main memory periodically. In all cases information will also have to be moved from main memory towards the cache, and generally via the bus or interconnection network, in order to meet the processor's need for code and data. Thus the cache does not reduce the *average* traffic on the bus, but helps to increase the peak performance of the processor.

- The *bus* or *interconnection network* is a key component of high performance architectures. For a large and fast system it can constitute a bottleneck, and therefore must be replaced in such cases by a 'non-blocking' network (such as the ones examined in Chapter 4) which allow each processor to access each memory bank quasi-simultaneously.

- The *operating system* is obviously not part of the architecture; however it has a major influence on system performance. In many multiprocessor systems, a specific processor is assigned to the operating system in order to reduce the time wasted in context-switching when system or hardware interrupts have to be handled. The consequence of this is that the corresponding processor tends to become a bottleneck which slows down the application being run on the other processors. Similar things can be said about the processor which handles secondary memory transfers or input−output operations.

We thus see that although they present the greatest potential for improved high performance computing, multiprocessor architectures also have intrinsic limitations which must be understood and mastered.

In general terms, we can estimate that the main technical problems which influence our capacity to make full use of the performance potential of multiprocessor architectures are:

- Parallel programming and program behaviour.

- Program preprocessing in order to extract parallelism, and operating system control to enhance parallel performance.

2.4. Different Types of Multiprocessors

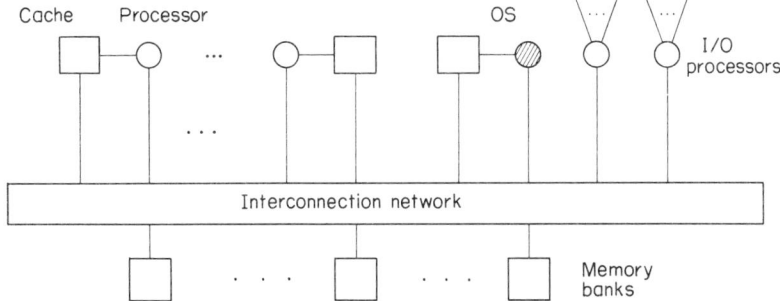

Figure 2.3: A conventional multiprocessor

- Communication problems including interprocess communication, cache and memory coherence or consistency, interconnection network and memory conflicts.

2.4 Different Types of Multiprocessors

In this section we shall enter into greater detail concerning different types of modern multiprocessor systems and discuss some of their performance characteristics. A classical multiprocessor architecture, which is similar to the one shown in Fig. 2.2, is given in Fig. 2.3. It is a system constructed around an interconnection network with an operating system processor (OS), two input–output (I/O) and secondary memory processors, and a set of ordinary processors equipped with cache memories.

The main appeal of this architecture is its simplicity and its relative similarity with a conventional centralized computer system. The main architectural difference with the latter, apart from the use of multiple processors, resides in the use of specific processors (which will often be based on the same microprocessor cards as the remaining processors) for operating system functions such as processor allocation, interrupt handling, memory management, etc., and for input–output operations and secondary memory access and transfers. This architecture clearly does rely on some 'centralized' system resources and in particular on these specialized processors and the interconnection network which can constitute the major bottleneck. Page faults and cache coherence problems will give rise to additional performance reduction.

In Fig. 2.4 we show an example of a *Hypercube architecture*. The system shown is composed of eight processors, one of which is specialized as the

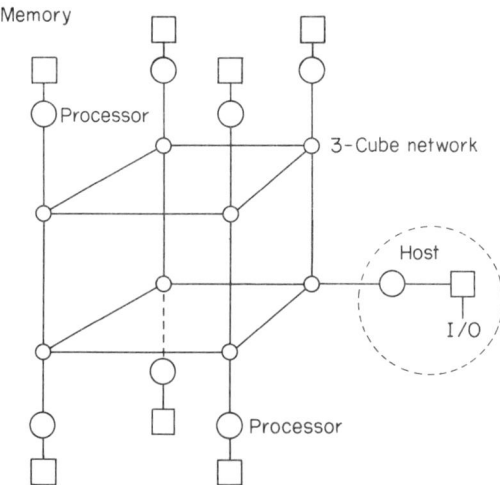

Figure 2.4: A Hypercube architecture

HOST or point of access and exit for the system as a whole. All processors here are physically equivalent and have a local memory accessible only by the processor. Contrary to the system of Fig. 2.3, the Hypercube is a distributed system machine, while the former is a shared memory machine. In certain respects a Hypercube is a distributed system which will generally use a level of granularity which is much coarser than that of a conventional multiprocessor. It can be used both as a SIMD and as a MIMD machine, where the 'I' in the term should be viewed as a complex *function* rather than as an *instruction*. Each processor will have to possess a copy in local memory of the essential portions of the operating system, except possibly for the file system and the input−output functions. The architecture gets its name from the communication architecture which is used; in the example shown we have a 3-cube. In general an n-cube machine will contain 2^n processors and each processor will be directly connected to n other processors (one in each dimension of the hyperspace) directly. Furthermore, each processor will be connected to any other processor in at most n hops or links. The non-existence of shared memory alleviates the network from the processor to memory (and vice versa) traffic. It implies however that all communication has to be carried out by the exchange of messages and therefore by the use of certain relatively slow operating system functions. Thus short messages are penalized because message initiation will take relatively long with respect to message delivery. In general applications which require the data to be shared or duplicated will not benefit from such architectures. The system will also be sensitive to process synchronization when the processes are being executed

2.4. Different Types of Multiprocessors

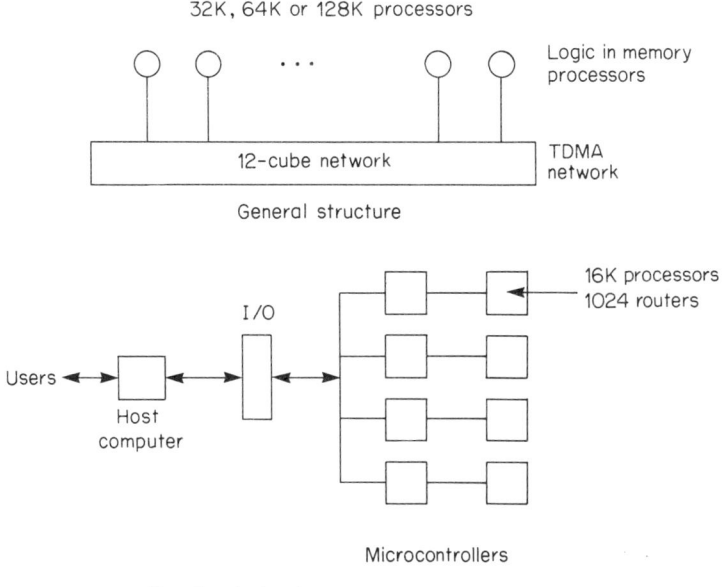

Figure 2.5: The Connection Machine

on different machines. However if special care is taken in the decomposition of the application it is known that Hypercubes can yield quasi-linear speed-up as a function of the number of processors [1].

Another novel architecture which uses a hypercube network for communication between processors is the *Connection Machine* (the name is a trade-mark of Thinking Machines Corporation). It is shown schematically in Fig. 2.5.

The Connection Machine is structured around a 12-cube interconnection network functioning in TDMA (time-division multiple access) mode; in each cycle of the network a processor can forward messages in twelve directions. The architecture is functionally structured around groups of 16K processors, each group receiving its execution information from a microcontroller. Each set of four processors within the 16K is interconnected by a NEWS network which handles local communications (NEWS stands for North−East−West−South), and these can share a single floating point arithmetic processor. Each normal processor has a small (4K, for instance) memory and can execute elementary non-numerical instructions. A very large computing capacity is obtained by the system which operates essentially in SIMD mode. Chapter 9 is devoted to the performance analysis of

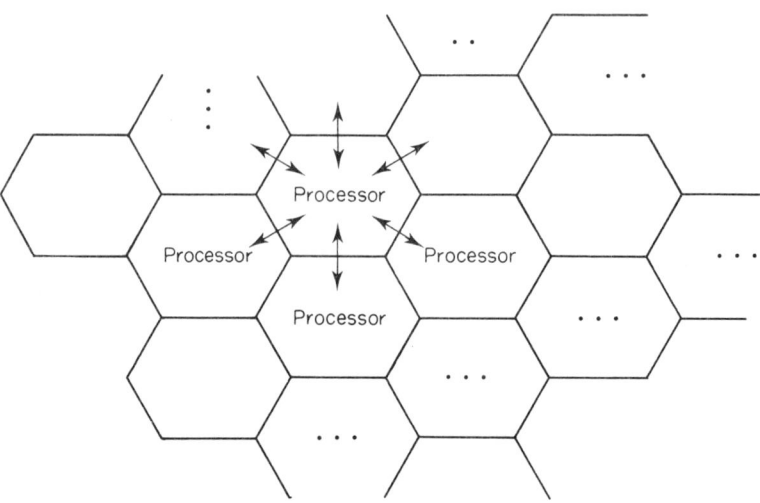

Figure 2.6: The lattice gas architecture

this architecture.

The last type of multiprocessor we shall discuss in this section is the *Lattice Gas Machine* [4]. Its functional structure is shown in Fig. 2.6 for a special case.

This architecture was conceived by physicists who wished to replace the conventional representation of gas dynamics by Navier-Stokes partial differential equations, by direct simulation of the interaction between molecules of the gas. Each processor of the machine is then assigned the task of simulating a set of molecules or a region of the space in which the molecules evolve. Theoretically such an approach can lead to an unlimited speed-up as a function of the number of processors being used, and for certain physical problems the local nature of interactions between molecules implies that each processor only has to interact with its adjacent neighbours. A similar idea could be used if one were simulating road traffic using a very large cellular multiprocessor. There are theoretical issues related to this approach to simulation. Indeed, in many cases the physical laws of local interaction are not completely understood, while macroscopic models (such as the Navier-Stokes equations) have been used and tested for a very long time. Another issue is related to the difficulty of introducing the effect of fields (action and influence at a distance) in such simulations because of the complexity of the communication network required and the inherent communication delays when a very

2.5. Conclusions

large number of processors is used. We would then be tempted to turn to a very expensive computer system such as the Connection Machine, rather than a very simple architecture such as the Lattice Gas Machine. However the idea is very appealing for many interesting applications.

2.5 Conclusions

In this chapter we have considered the main advantages and shortcomings of different classes of parallel processing systems. We have indicated that multiprocessors present the greatest promise regarding the potential for increased performance. We have then reviewed different types of multiprocessor architectures and have discussed their merits and limitations with respect to system performance.

One major issue we have not addressed is that of the influence of the internal structure of the application programs which is bound to have a profound influence on performance. This matter is addressed in Chapter 3 at a global level, and then in Chapters 5, 6, 7 at a greater level of detail. In Chapter 4 efficient communication networks will be discussed, and their performance will be analysed.

2.6 Bibliography

The concept of a scalable problem, i.e. one in which the speed-up (or ratio of run-time with one processor to the run-time with N processors) increases linearly in N, is illustrated on a Hypercube machine in [1]. Earlier results from the late 1970s and early 1980s concerning different types of parallel architectures are presented in [3]. The basic ideas related to the Connection Machine are presented in [4, 5]. The Lattice Gas Machine principles are discussed in [6, 7, 8].

[1] Gustafson, J. L. 'Reevaluating Amdahl's Law', *Communications of the ACM*, Vol. 31, No. 5, pp. 532– 533 (1988).

[2] Cosnard, M., Robert, Y. and Tourancheau, B. 'Evaluating Speed-ups on Distributed Memory Architectures', to appear in *Parallel Computing*.

[3] Rodrigue, G. *Parallel Computations*, Academic Press, New York, USA (1982).

[4] Hillis, W. D. *The Connection Machine*, The MIT Press, Cambridge, Mass., USA (1985).

[5] Thinking Machines Corporation, 'Connection Machine Model CM-2 Technical Summary', *Technical Report HA87-4*, Cambridge, Mass., USA (April 1987).

[6] Hardy, J., Depazzis, O. and Pomeau, Y. 'Molecular Dynamics of a Classical Lattice Gas: Transport Properties and Time Correlation Functions', *Phys. Rev.*, Vol. A13, pp. 1949–1961 (1976).

[7] Frisch, U., D'Humieres, D., Hasslacher, B., Lallemand, P., Pomeau, Y. and Rivet, J.P. 'Lattice Gas Hydrodynamics in Two and Three Dimensions', *Complex Systems*, Vol. 1, pp. 649–707 (1987).

[8] Clouquer, A. and D'Humieres, D. 'R.A.P., A Family of Cellular Automaton Machines for Free Dynamics', *Helvetica Physica Acta*, Vol.62, pp. 525–544 (1989).

3

Multiprocessor Speed-up and Amdahl's Law

3.1 Introduction

Consider a set of programs that is to be executed on a multiprocessor containing N identical processors. Each of these processors may itself be equipped with one or more array processors attached for its private use.

Amdahl's law [1, 2] estimates an upper bound of $N/(1 + CN)$ for the actual speed-up, or ratio of elapsed time with a single processor to the elapsed execution time with N processors. Recent experiments [3] have shown that this may be an unnecessarily pessimistic estimate of speed-up and that values close to N may be obtained for specific applications.

Amdahl's argument [1, 2] is the following. Consider a program which is executed in some time E on a single processor. Assume now that N identical processors are provided; the execution time will now be E/N if the program can be cut into N parallel components each of which is executed in the same amount of time. However there will in general be some time, say C' spent in communication between parts of the program. Thus the total effective execution in parallel will be $(C' + E/N)$, and the speed-up will then be the ratio of the execution time with a single processor to the ratio of the execution time with N processors, or

$$\frac{E}{\frac{E}{N} + C'} = \frac{N}{1 + CN}, \qquad C = \frac{C'}{E}$$

We derive in Chapters 5 and 6 another approach to computing the estimated maximum speed-up [4] assuming an unlimited number of processors, based on a model which considers the density p of precedence relations between tasks in programs. In Chapter 6 we obtain an approximate formula $(1+p)/2p$ for the *maximum* speed-up, on the average, for such a family of programs assuming that the number of processors available is unlimited. When p is close to 1, nearly all tasks are interdependent and the programs will in fact execute sequentially; the speed-up factor itself will be close to just 1. On the other hand, when p is very close to 0 we are dealing with programs composed of many quasi-independent tasks and the maximum speed-up is very large. An 'infinite' speed-up merely means that the average execution time for the program family remains nearly constant as the number of individual tasks in the program becomes very large.

In this chapter we shall begin by considering Amdahl's law and suggest some modifications or amendments that can serve to explain speed-up factors which are nearly linear in the number of processors. We shall then return to the intrinsic processor independent behaviour of parallel programs and introduce a new model of parallel program behaviour, the *Activity Set Model*,[1] which may be used to describe the behaviour of parallel programs and to derive bounds to the speed-up which can be expected when such programs are executed on multiprocessors.

We first consider a simple amendment to Amdahl's law, and derive a speed-up formula with N processors which is of the form

$$\frac{N}{[(1-\epsilon)(1+\delta) + \epsilon \, \log_2 N]}$$

where ϵ is the probability that the programs *cannot* effectively use N processors. δ is a measure of the *imbalance* between the workloads of each processor when N processors are used. Indeed δ/N is the amount of time in *excess* of the optimistic equal run-time $1/N$ which the most loaded processor will take to run the task which has been assigned to it. Thus, when the computation has been organized so that ϵ is very small, the speed-up can be as high as $N/(1+\delta)$. These results are detailed in Section 3.2.

In Section 3.3, we consider an evaluation of speed-up based on intrinsic program behaviour which leads to general bounds.

Throughout the discussion we consider a program, or a family of programs, whose average run-time on a single process is equal to 1.

---

[1]The name of this model is, of course, inspired by Peter Denning's Process Working Set Model used in paging. Alan Batson introduced many years ago the term Activity Set in the context of segmented memory management; the term is used here in another sense.

3.2 An Amendment to Amdahl's Law

Assume that the program, or family of programs, considered makes full use of the N processors with probability $(1 - \epsilon)$. It will use only i processors $(1 \leq i \leq N - 1)$ with probability ϵ_i, where

$$\epsilon = \sum_{i=1}^{N-1} \epsilon_i$$

If it uses N processors, one of these will have the greatest workload so that the run-time of the program on N processors is given by the time elapsed for the most heavily loaded one, or

$$\frac{1}{N} + \frac{\delta}{N}$$

Obviously, if all the processors' workload were perfectly balanced the elapsed time would be simply $1/N$.

Similarly when only i processors are used the elapsed time will be

$$\frac{1}{i} + \frac{\delta_i}{i}$$

These times should be viewed as average values when a *family* of programs is considered.

Thus the average elapsed time when N processors are available is given by the formula

$$T(N) = (1 - \epsilon)\left(\frac{1}{N} + \frac{\delta}{N}\right) + \sum_{1}^{N-1} \epsilon_i \left(\frac{1}{i} + \frac{\delta_i}{i}\right) \tag{3.1}$$

So that the speed-up $T(1)/T(N) = 1/T(N)$ is simply given by

$$S = \frac{N}{\left[(1 - \epsilon)(1 + \delta) + N \sum_{1}^{N-1} \epsilon_i \left(\frac{1}{i} + \frac{\delta_i}{i}\right)\right]} \tag{3.2}$$

3.2.1 The Most Favourable Case

Naturally, the greatest speed-up will be obtained if we set $\epsilon_{N-1} = \epsilon, \epsilon_i = 0$ for $(1 \leq i \leq N - 2)$.

We then have for large enough N:

$$S \cong \frac{N}{1 + \delta(1 - \epsilon) + \delta_{N-1}} \tag{3.3}$$

This formula explains the quasi-linear speed-ups which can be encountered for some specific applications.

3.2.2 The Least Favourable Case

We may consider that the least favourable case for a family of programs is obtained by setting

$$\epsilon_i = 1 - \epsilon = 1/N, \qquad \text{for all } 1 \leq i \leq N-1$$

which implies that we are equally likely to make use of any number of processors; this is the assumption made in Amdahl's law. We then have

$$S = \frac{N}{\sum_1^N \frac{1}{i} + \sum_1^N \frac{\delta_i}{i}}, \qquad \delta_N = \delta$$

Since $\sum_1^N \frac{1}{i} \geq \log_2 N$, we have

$$S \leq \frac{N}{\log_2 N} \tag{3.4}$$

3.2.3 Amendment to Amdahl's Law when Communication is Neglected

Let us consider a family of programs which can fully use all N processors with probability $1 - \epsilon$. If a program in this family cannot make full use, then it is equally likely to use $N-1$, $N-2$, ..., or just one processor. We then have $\epsilon_i = \epsilon/(N-1)$, $(1 \leq i \leq N-1)$ so that we obtain

$$S \leq \frac{N}{\left[(1-\epsilon)(1+\delta) + \frac{\epsilon N}{N-1}(\log_2(N-1) + \sum_1^{N-1} \frac{\delta_i}{i})\right]}$$

$$S \leq \frac{N}{(1-\epsilon)(1+\delta) + \epsilon \log_2 N}, \qquad \text{for large } N \tag{3.5}$$

We may consider this bound as a useful compromise between the favourable situation described in Section 3.2.1 and the excessively pessimistic bound provided in Section 3.2.2.

3.2.4 The effect of Communication Time between Parallel Processors

In the preceding discussion, the effect of the communication time between parallel processes has not been explicitly considered. Let us now turn to this important element.

Suppose now that when a program is effectively run with i processors, a total communication time $c(i)$ will be spent. This time can be observed relatively easily on message passing architectures such as the Hypercube [9, 10]. It will exist in general because the parallel processes constituting an application program have to communicate with each other in general. Thus the total execution time of a program using N processors now takes the following form:

$$T'(N) = (1-\epsilon)\left(\frac{1}{N} + \frac{\delta}{N} + c(N)\right) + \sum_{1}^{N-1} \epsilon_i \left(\frac{1}{i} + \frac{\delta_i}{i} + c(i)\right)$$

which is an extension of (3.1).

Using the same arguments as in Section 3.2.3 we obtain the following formula for the speed-up:

$$S \leq \frac{N}{(1-\epsilon)(1+\delta) + Nc(N) + \epsilon \log_2 N}$$

Assume now that exactly N processors are effectively used; the speed-up then becomes

$$S = \frac{N}{1 + \delta + Nc(N)} \tag{3.6}$$

In general, $c(N)$ will not decrease as N increases. Indeed often the contrary may be the case for obvious practical reasons. Thus for large values of N, $c(N)$ will be the limiting factor to the speed-up, since

$$S \approx \frac{1}{c(N)}, \quad \text{for very large } N.$$

3.3 A Model of Intrinsic Program Behaviour

Consider a program which is being executed with an unlimited number of processors. Its behaviour may be characterized by a variable $n(t)$ representing the number of active processes or tasks at some instant t, lying between the instant $t = 0$ when the program execution is initiated and the instant $t = T$ when it ends. Such a behaviour is shown in Fig. 3.1. $n(t)$ is the *size* of the Activity Set at time t.

The total work

$$W = \int_0^T n(t) \, dt \tag{3.7}$$

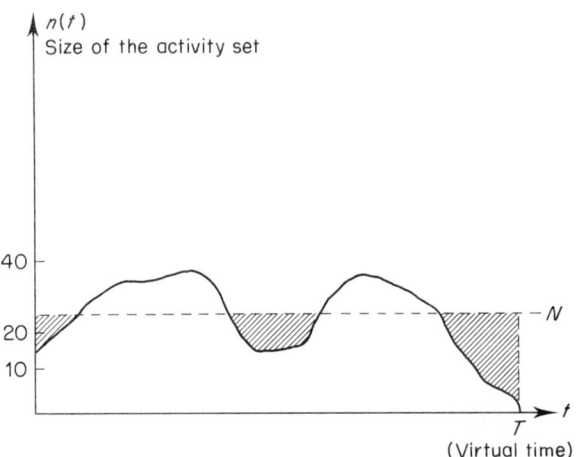

Figure 3.1: Size of the Activity Set of parallel program as a function of virtual time t, between $t = 0$ when the program execution begins and $t = T$ when it ends

represents the amount of computational effort which must be accomplished by a set of processors in order to execute the program.

The *Activity Set* of the program at time t is the set of parallel processes or tasks that are running simultaneously at time t.

The *parallelism index* N_0:

$$N_0 = \frac{1}{T} \int_0^T n(t)\mathrm{d}t = W/T \qquad (3.8)$$

is the average number of active processes in the program, or the average number of processors which it can use simultaneously.

Time t in the expressions above should be considered to be the virtual time, or program execution time from which the time spent for all interruptions (paging, I/O, other programs' execution time, etc.) has been deleted.

If the program is to be run on a single processor whose speed is c times faster than any one of the initial set of processors, the program will now run in time

$$T(c,1) = W/c = N_0 T/c \qquad (3.9)$$

If, on the other hand, we are limited to running the program on N processors, each of which has the same power as one of the processors in the initial unlimited set, we can derive some bounds on the execution time.

3.3. A Model of Intrinsic Program Behaviour

Consider the quantity

$$C(N) = \int_0^T (N - n(t))^+ \, dt$$

where

$$(x)^+ = \begin{cases} x, & \text{if } x \geq 0 \\ 0, & \text{if } x < 0 \end{cases}$$

$C(N)$ denotes the amount of additional work which N processors could provide during the interval $[0, T]$, or their excess capacity, when the program is executed with an unlimited number of processors. It is shown as the shaded area of Figure 3.1. Similarly,

$$D(N) = \int_0^T (n(t) - N)^+ \, dt$$

is the work accomplished by the other processors being used when the total number of processors available is unlimited.

Ideally, when the total number of processors is limited to N, the total execution time $T(N)$ cannot be smaller than

$$T(N) \geq T + (D(N) - C(N))^+ / N$$

since in the best case the excess capacity $C(N)$ will be used to accommodate as much excess work $D(N)$ as the processors can take.

Similarly, an upper bound to $T(N)$ can be derived by considering that all of the work $D(N)$ will be accomplished on the N processors after time T:

$$T(N) \leq T + D(N)/N$$

The speed-up obtained by using N processors instead of a single processor (of speed $c = 1$) can now be estimated from these bounds. It is given by the formula $S = T(1)/T(N)$ so that

$$\frac{N_0 T}{T + \frac{(D(N) - C(N))^+}{N}} \geq S \geq \frac{N_0 T}{T + D(N)/N} \qquad (3.10)$$

or

$$\frac{N_0 N}{N + \frac{(D(N) - C(N))^+}{T}} \geq S \geq \frac{N_0 N}{N + D(N)/T} \qquad (3.11)$$

From these inequalities we see quite clearly that S can never exceed N_0, which should be obvious, but also that it is bounded from above by the multiplicative factor

$$\frac{1}{1 + \frac{(D(N) - C(N))^+}{NT}}$$

and from below by the multiplicative factor

$$\frac{1}{1 + \frac{D(N)}{NT}}$$

3.3.1 A Statistical Interpretation

Clearly, the precise behaviour of a program as given by the function $n(t)$ is in general very difficult to predict since it will obviously be data dependent. Thus it is quite natural to treat $n(t)$ as a random function so that N_0, $D(N)/T$, $C(N)/T$ will now have convenient statistical interpretations in terms of the statistical average or expected value $E[\cdot]$ taken over the finite time interval $[0, T]$:

$$N_0 \rightarrow E[n(t)]$$
$$\frac{D(N)}{T} \rightarrow E[(n(t) - N)^+]$$
$$\frac{C(N)}{T} \rightarrow E[(N - n(t))^+]$$

We shall now write in particular

$$\frac{S}{N_0} \geq \frac{1}{1 + \frac{1}{N}E[(n(t) - N)^+]} \quad (3.12)$$

3.3.2 A Numerical Example

Within the framework of the statistical interpretation of $n(t)$, consider the case where it is time independent and its distribution function is geometric over the interval $[0, T]$:

$$P[n(t) = i] = q^{i-1}(1 - q), \quad i \geq 1$$

This example describes a situation in which the program is always more likely to have a *smaller* number of active parallel tasks. Clearly, q must be chosen so that $E[n(t)] = N_0$, hence $N_0 = 1/(1 - q)$ or $q = (N_0 - 1)/N_0$.

3.4. Conclusions

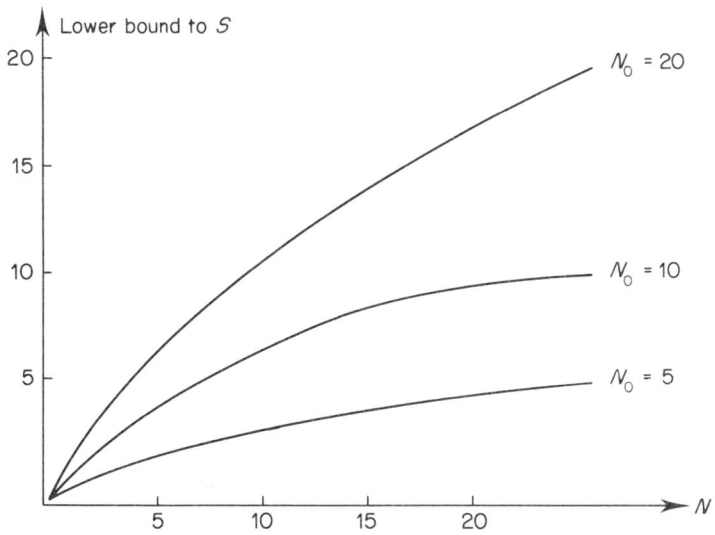

Figure 3.2: The lower bound for the speed-up S as a function of N for various values of N_0 provided by equation (3.13)

We then have

$$E[(n(t) - N)^+] = \sum_{i=N}^{\infty}(i - N)q^{i-1}(1 - q)$$

$$= q^N/(1-q) = \left(\frac{N_0 - 1}{N_0}\right)^N \cdot N_0$$

Hence

$$\frac{S}{N_0} \geq \frac{1}{1 + \frac{N_0}{N}\left(\frac{N_0-1}{N_0}\right)^N} \qquad (3.13)$$

In Fig. 3.2 we show the lower bound (3.13) to the speed-up S as a function of the number of processors N for various values of N_0 (the parallelism index).

3.4 Conclusions

In this chapter we have considered some amendments to Amdahl's law which take into account the fact the programs may be able to make effective use of all of the processors which are available to them, but which also recognize the fact that imbalance in the partition of the workload between processors reduces the speed-up one could expect. We have then suggested examining the speed-up issue in terms of a representation of the intrinsic behavior of parallel program execution which we call the Activity Set Model. This model describes the set of simultaneously active parallel processes as a function of program virtual time. We show how the size of the Activity Set can be used to derive bounds on the speed-up of the programs as a function of the number of processors which are available to it.

3.5 Bibliography

Amdahl's law has been introduced in [1]. A more recent discussion of the problem and some pertinent modifications can be found in [2]. Other relevant references and extensions can be found in [5, 6, 7, 8, 9]. Most of the material in this chapter is new however.

[1] Amdahl, G. M. 'Validity of the Single-Processor Approach to Achieving Large-Scale Computing Capabilities', *AFIPS Conference Proceedings 30*, AFIPS Press, pp. 483–485 (1967).

[2] Gustafson, J. L.'Reevaluating Amdahl's Law', *Communications of the ACM* **31, 5**, pp. 532–533 (1988).

[3] Cosnard, M., Robert, Y. and Tourancheau, B. 'Evaluating Speed-ups on Distributed Memory Architectures', to appear in *Parallel Computing*.

[4] Gelenbe, E., Nelson, R., Philips, T. and Tantawi, A. 'Asymptotic Processing Time of a Model of Parallel Computation', *Proceedings National Computer Conference*, USA (November 1986).

[5] Gustafson, J.L. 'The Scaled-sized Model: A Revision of Amdahl's Law', *ICS Supercomputing ' 88*, L.P. Kartashev and S.I. Kartashev (eds), International Supercomputing Institute Inc. Vol.II, pp. 130–133 (1988).

[6] Gustafson, J.L., Hawkinson, S. and Scott, K. 'The Architecture of a Homogeneous Vector Supercomputer', *Proceedings of ICCP 86*, IEEE Computer Society Press, pp. 649–652 (1986).

3.5. Bibliography

[7] Moler, C. 'Matrix Computations on Distributed Memory Multiprocessors', *Hypercube Multiprocessors 1986*, M.T. Heath (ed.), SIAM Editions, pp. 161–180 (1986).

[8] Robert, Y. and Tourancheau, B., 'LU and QR Factorization on the FPS T Series Hypercube', *CONPAR 88*, Manchester, UK (September 1988).

[9] Saad, Y. 'Gaussian Elimination on Hypercubes', *Parallel Algorithms and Architectures*, M. Cosnard et al. (eds), North-Holland, pp. 5–17 (1986).

4

Performance of Interconnection Networks

4.1 Introduction

In the previous chapter it was stated that the main limitation to the increase in performance of a conventional multiprocessor architecture with common memory as the number of processors and memory banks are allowed to increase, i.e. as the raw processing power of the system is increased, resides in the communication delays between the processors and the shared memory.

Indeed, as the processing power of the system is increased either as a consequence of an increase in the number of simultaneously active processors or as a result of an increase in the number of instructions which are executed per unit time, the demands placed on the system used to interconnect the processors and the memory also increases. At some point, the interconnection system can become the main bottleneck of the architecture. It is therefore important to have tools which can be used to evaluate rapidly and accurately the performance of the interconnection network.

In this chapter we shall present a mathematical tool that can be used to predict the performance of a large class of interconnection networks such as the Omega, Flip, Indirect Binary Cube, Baseline networks. All of these networks are topologically equivalent to the Baseline network shown in Fig. 4.1.

As indicated in the bibliography at the end of this chapter, such interconnection systems and their performance have received considerable attention due to the important role they play in the design of effective multiproces-

34   4. Performance of Interconnection Networks

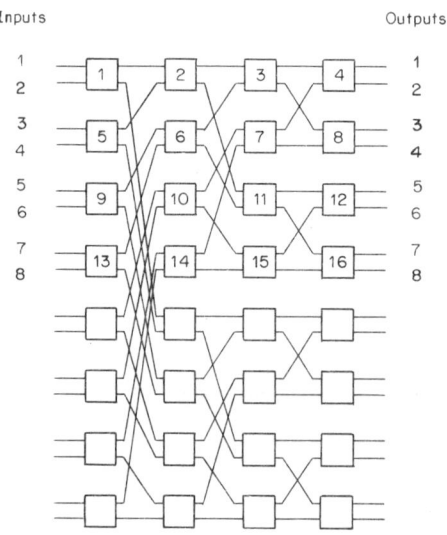

Figure 4.1: The Baseline network

sor architectures [1, 9, 13, 14]. However their very large size as well as the small values of the network blocking probabilities which are being sought make them very difficult to simulate. Indeed, the simulation runs needed for accurate estimation in this context will tend to be excessively long. It is well known that exact mathematical modelling techniques are difficult to use, for similar reasons, in this context. Thus in this chapter we present an approximate but validated analysis methodology and establish its high degree of accuracy.

Such a network has N inputs (the processors) and N outputs (the memory boxes), where for some n we have $N = 2^n$. Each of the processors can be connected to any memory along a unique path which traverses a set of binary switches shown as boxes in Fig. 4.1. Each box can give rise to four distinct interconnections between its pair of inputs and its pair of outputs. However each input of each box can be connected at a given instant to only *one* of its two inputs. This can lead to conflicts in establishing paths between different inputs and outputs. In order to illustrate such conflicts, let us turn to Fig. 4.1.

Suppose we wish to interconnect input 1 to output 5. The interconnection path will traverse boxes 1, 2, 11, 12. Notice that there is a unique path going

4.1. Introduction

from input 1 to output 5. Notice also that to establish this path we must connect the *upper input* of box 2 to its *lower output*.

Suppose now that we also wish to interconnect input 3 to output 7. This path will have to traverse boxes 5, 2, 11, 16. However it will conflict with the previous path at box 2, since it needs to establish a link between its *lower input* and its *lower output*, and the latter is already occupied by the path 1, 2, 11, 12.

Such conflicts may be alleviated if the communication in the interconnection network takes place in 'packet switching' mode. In this case no permanent connections are established in the network and information is carried in the form of short packets each of which is routed dynamically. The disadvantage of this approach is that buffers have to be provided at each switch for packets which may have to wait and packet construction and reassembly hardware must be included at the input and output of the network, respectively.

We shall assume in this chapter that the network operates in the more conventional 'circuit switching' mode. In this approach a processor requesting access to a memory will in fact request the establishment of the complete path from input to output. The access from processor to memory will only occur when the path is established. When the access terminates, the path is released.

In circuit switching mode, two approaches can be taken to the establishment of circuits:

- the DROP approach, which stops the attempt to establish a circuit as soon as a conflict is detected at one of the switches on the path,

- the HOLD approach which reserves all of the switches for which there is no conflict, up to the one where a conflict is detected, until this particular switch becomes free; when this happens the establishment of the path is pursued until all necessary switches are obtained.

Both approaches will be examined in this chapter.

From the above discussion it may appear that we are concerned only with transfers from the processors towards memory. Of course this is not the case since the networks we consider can provide a two-way communication channel between processor and memory once the path is established.

Our purpose here is not to provide a survey of interconnection networks for multiprocessor systems. A useful reference for this is [5]. Other relevant references are mentioned in the last section of this chapter. We concentrate on the performance of Baseline networks, and hence on networks which are their topological and functional equivalents because they have a particularly desirable feature with respect to the limitation of conflicts between paths.

Indeed let i denote the level of a switch: e.g. switch 1 is of level 1, while 6 is of level 2, etc. The level of a switch is simply the number of switches, including itself, which separate it from the processors. We see that a level i switch's input is connected to exactly 2^i inputs or processors, and any one of its two input lines is connected to 2^{i-1} processors. Similarly, any processor will be connected to 2^{i-1} inputs of switches at level i and hence to 2^i distinct output lines. Thus the Baseline network spreads out in an optimal fashion, on the average, the traffic from the processors by sharing it evenly between switches at each level.

The main measure of interest for interconnection networks is the *bandwidth* which we denote BW. It is the number of *accesses* which the network will satisfy per unit time. Of course the BW will be obtained under certain assumptions concerning, for instance, the number of requests per unit time and the length of each access. In Sections 4.2, 4.3 and 4.4 we shall evaluate the Baseline network for the DROP operating assumption, while Section 4.5 will be devoted to the HOLD assumption. Both numerical results concerning the BW based on the mathematical models, and simulation results will be presented. We shall see that the models we exhibit yield very accurate predictions and that they may therefore be used in various practical situations.

4.2 Bandwidth of the Baseline and Omega Networks with the Drop Approach

The behaviour of a processor with respect to the network may be represented by the state transition diagram shown in Fig. 4.2 for the DROP approach. Here the processor requests a path by formulating requests for access to the set of switches along that path. If it cannot obtain a switch, it abandons its request at that point (i.e. it drops it) and will try again at some later date.

On Fig 4.2, state 0 represents some processor in quiescent state, while state $n + 1$ represents an ongoing successful access. State b represents the processor when it has dropped its request.

Since a path is of length n, the processor will be in some state i $(1 \leq i \leq n)$, if it has successfully obtained the first i switches on its path. From state

4.2. Bandwidth of the Baseline and Omega Networks ...

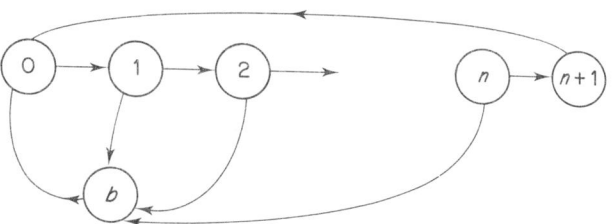

Figure 4.2: State transition diagram for a processor with the DROP approach

i it will go to b if its $(i+1)$-th request was not successful, otherwise it will go to state $(i+1)$, for $(1 \leq i \leq n)$. From state 0 it will go to state 1 when it decides to request a memory access. From state n it will go to $n+1$ if all of the switch requests it has made are satisfied. Finally, when it has completed its access it goes from state $n+1$ to state 0 and releases the path.

We shall denote by $1/\lambda_0$ the average time spent by the processor in state 0 before making a request. Thus λ_o is the rate at which a quiescent processor makes requests. When the processor is in some state $(i = 1, ..., n-1)$, we assume it requests the next switch after an average time T_i, with a probability of success q_i. In practice T_i will usually be much smaller than $1/\lambda_o$, and q_i will depend on the traffic conditions. We shall use the following notation for $(i = 1, ..., n-1)$:

$$\lambda_i = q_i/T_i, \qquad \mu_i = (1-q_i)/T_i \qquad (4.1)$$

Usually all the T_i's will be identical so that with $\mu = 1/T_i$. T_n will be the time necessary to establish the access to memory once all switches have been obtained (with $\lambda_n = 1/T_n$) and $1/\phi_s$ will be the average duration of the access, after which the processor will return to state 0. $1/\phi_b$ will denote the average time spent in state b, after a conflict is detected, before the processor returns to the quiescent state.

From these assumptions and without making any restrictions on the distribution of the times we have defined, we can obtain the steady-state probabilities π_i associated with the states of the model from the following equations for the semi-Markov model we have used:

$$\begin{aligned}
\lambda \pi_0 &= \phi_s \pi_{n+1} + \phi_b \pi_b \\
\mu \pi_1 &= \lambda \pi_o \\
\mu \pi_i &= \lambda_{i-1} \pi_{i-1}, \qquad \forall i = 2, n \\
\phi_s \pi_{n+1} &= \lambda_n \pi_n
\end{aligned} \qquad (4.2)$$

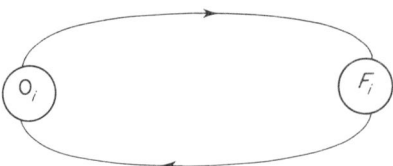

Figure 4.3: States of an output line of a switch at level i

$$\phi_b \pi_b = \sum_{i=1}^{n} \mu_i \pi_i$$

This model which represents the behaviour of any processor with respect to the network is completed by another model which represents the state of interconnections within the network.

Consider a level i switch, and in particular the state of one of its two output lines; the output line state will be O_i if it is occupied and F_i if it is free. We shall model its behaviour as a two-state process as shown on Fig. 4.3.

If we denote by $1/\tau_i$ the average time spent by the line in state O_i and $1/\varepsilon_i$ the average time spent in state F_i, we easily obtain the probabilities $P(O_i)$, $P(F_i)$ associated with each state

$$P(O_i) = \frac{\varepsilon_i}{\tau_i} P(F_i) \tag{4.3}$$

$$P(O_i) = \frac{\varepsilon_i}{\varepsilon_i + \tau_i} \tag{4.4}$$

These probabilities will be used to relate the transition of the processor state to the availability of the output lines. We shall thus have from (4.1) and (4.4.):

$$1 - q_i = P(O_i)$$

so that

$$\mu_i = \mu \varepsilon_i / (\varepsilon_i + \tau_i) \tag{4.5}$$

We can also relate the ε_i to the behaviour of each processor. Indeed, the passage from F_i to O_i implies that some processor goes from state i to state $i+1$. As shown in Fig. 4.4, the connection between any two successive levels may be attempted by *one* processsor in one of the *three* situations indicated.

4.2. Bandwidth of the Baseline and Omega Networks ... 39

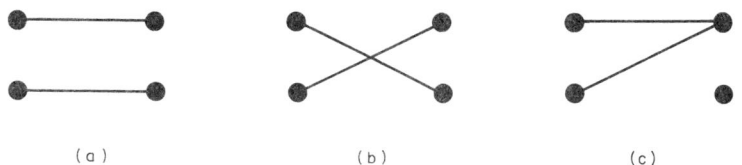

Figure 4.4: Three different interconnection situations for a processor

On Fig 4.4, for each of the three interconnection diagrams representing the internal interconnection attempts of a switch assuming that the input line above the figures is already connected, while the input line below is used by the processor being considered, we see that the first two interconnection patterns (a) and (b) are successful, while (c) will lead to a failure. Assuming all three patterns equally likely, since they only depend on the memory box which the processor needs to access, we shall have

$$\varepsilon_i = \frac{2}{3}\lambda_i \pi_i = \frac{2}{3} q_i \mu \pi_i \qquad (4.6)$$

since ε_i is the rate at which the line goes from the free state to the occupied state. The rate τ_i at which the level i output line goes from state 0_i to F_i will be a consequence of one of the two following events:

- blocking occurred at a higher level, so this line is released,
- the processor releases the path at the end of an access.

We then have

$$\tau_i = \sum_{j=i+1}^{n} \frac{\pi_j \mu_j}{\sum_{j=i+1}^{n} \pi_j} + \frac{\pi_{n+1}\phi_s}{\sum_{j=i+1}^{n} \pi_j} \qquad (4.7)$$

Notice that for the line to go from state 0_i to F_i it is necessary that the processor be in some state $j > i$; hence all the probabilities which appear in (4.7) are conditioned on this event. Using (4.5), (4.6) and (4.7) we can write

$$\mu_i = \mu \frac{\lambda_i \pi_i}{\lambda_i \pi_i + \frac{3}{2} \frac{\phi_s \pi_{n+1} + \sum_{j=i+1}^{n} \pi_j \mu_j}{\sum_{j=i+1}^{n} \pi_j}} \qquad (4.8)$$

The bandwidth is now the rate at which processor accesses are satisfied, or equivalently the rate at which they are completed:

$$BW = 2^n \pi_{n+1} \phi_s \qquad (4.9)$$

so that the main quantity of interest for which we must obtain a solution is π_{n+1}.

4.3 Numerical Solution of the DROP Model

In order to obtain π_{n+1}, we have to solve the system of equations presented above which relates the unknown variables π_i to the unknown variables μ_i as summarized in (4.8) with the additional equation

$$\sum_{i=0}^{n+1} \pi_i + \pi_b = 1 \qquad (4.10)$$

The known or given quantities are μ, ϕ_s, ϕ_b.

From equations (4.2) and (4.7), after some algebra, we obtain

$$\lambda_n = \frac{\mu}{1 + \frac{2\pi_{n+1}}{3}}$$

$$\pi_n = \frac{\pi_{n+1}}{\lambda_n} \phi_s$$

Similarly, using (4.2) in (4.7) we can write

$$\lambda_i = \mu - \frac{\mu^2 \pi_{i+1}}{\mu \pi_{i+1} + \frac{3}{2}\left[\frac{\phi_s \pi_{n+1} + \sum_{j=i+1}^{n}(\mu - \lambda_j)\pi_j}{\sum_{j=i+1}^{n} \pi_j}\right]}$$

for $(1 \leq i \leq n)$. Using the third equation in (4.2) we can write

$$\sum_{j=i+1}^{n}(\mu - \lambda_j)\pi_j = \sum_{j=i+1}^{n} \mu\pi_j - \sum_{j=i+2}^{n} \mu\pi_j - \phi_s \pi_{n+1}$$
$$= \mu \pi_{i+1} - \phi_s \pi_{n+1}$$

hence the expression for λ_i simplifies to

$$\lambda_i = \mu - \frac{\mu^2 \pi_{i+1}}{\mu \pi_{i+1} + \frac{3}{2} \frac{\mu \pi_{i+1}}{\sum_{j=i+1}^{n} \pi_j}}$$
$$= \mu - \frac{\mu}{1 + \frac{3}{2}\left(\sum_{j=i+1}^{n} \pi_j\right)^{-1}}$$

yielding
$$\lambda_i = \frac{3\mu}{3 + 2\sum_{j=i+1}^{n} \pi_j}, \qquad 1 \leq i \leq n$$

Again using the third equation in (4.2) we end up with the following polynomial in the π_i's ; for ($1 \leq i \leq n$):

$$\pi_i = \frac{\mu \pi_{i+1}}{\lambda_i} = \pi_{i+1}\left(1 + \frac{2}{3}\sum_{j=i+1}^{n+1} \pi_j\right) \tag{4.11}$$

which will constitute the basis for the numerical solution method we use to obtain the π_i's. π_0 and π_b are simply related to the other probabilities by:

$$\pi_0 = \frac{\mu \pi_1}{\lambda}$$
$$\pi_b = \frac{1}{\phi_b}[\mu \pi_1 - \phi_s \pi_{n+1}] \tag{4.12}$$

4.4 Bandwidth of the DROP Model

It can be shown that the solution of the system of equations (4.12), with the normalizing condition (4.10), exists and is unique; this will not be done here. We shall examine numerical results concerning the bandwidth BW of the network, and we shall validate the results based on our mathematical model using simulations. For all cases considered, the simulations confirm our analytical model predictions within less than 4 percent error.

In Fig. 4.5 we plot the bandwidth of the DROP network as a function of the load λ imposed by each processor. Without loss of generality we take $\phi_s = 1$ so that the time unit is the average time necessary for a memory access $1 = 1/\phi_s$. Thus we vary λ from 0.1 (light load) to 1 (heavy load). We choose $\mu = 0.1$, so that we are dealing with a network which is relatively slow in establishing the connection between a processor and the memory bank it requests. We have taken $\phi_b = 1$ so that the release time in case of blocking is the same, on the average, as the memory access time. We see that as the load increases, the bandwidth increases much less than linearly.

In Fig. 4.6 we compare analytical and simulation results in order to evaluate the accuracy of the analytical model for a network with $n = 4$ and $n = 5$. The quantity tabulated is π_{n+1} which enters into the formula for the bandwidth, since $BW = 2^n \phi_s \pi_{n+1}$. The system being simulated is the actual interconnection network, and the parameters chosen correspond to a network in which data is actually transferred as the path is being established: $\phi_s \gg \mu$. Excellent agreement is observed between the two approaches.

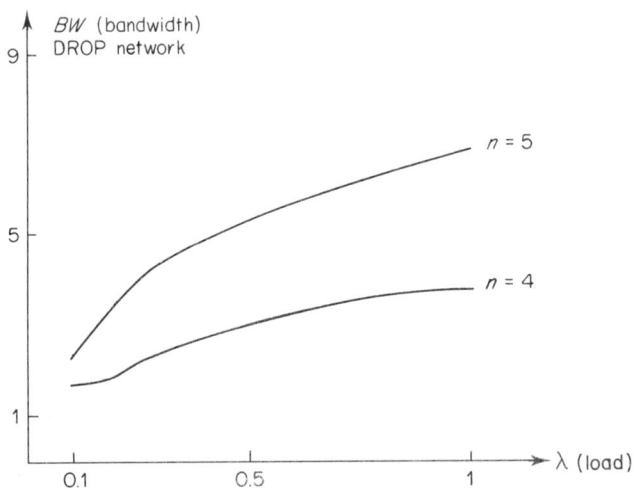

Figure 4.5: Bandwidth as a function of load for the DROP network

4.5 The HOLD Network Model

The HOLD network functions on the principle that when a circuit is being established, if at level i the request for the next level cannot be satisfied because the line is already taken, then the circuit is put on hold; all connections established so far on the path are maintained until the next level connection is freed. At that point the establishment of the circuit is pursued. This approach is less wasteful of the time of a processor which is making an attempt at establishing a circuit. It may be less efficient in terms of the usage of the network since a path is held even when it is not being used. The establishment of a circuit or path in the HOLD network is shown by the state transition diagram of Fig. 4.7.

State 0 represents the quiescent state of the processor. In state i, ($1 \leq i \leq n$), the processor is *requesting* a connection at the i-th level. If this succeeds it proceeds to state $i+1$; otherwise it enters state B_i in which it remains until it does succeed to enter state $i+1$. In state $n+1$ the processor is actually accessing the memory, after which it enters state 0.

As for the DROP model, we shall denote by μ the rate at which an attempt is made in state i to obtain a connection. We shall have

$$\mu = \lambda_i + \mu_i, \qquad 1 \leq i \leq n$$

4.5. The HOLD Network Model

$\mu = 1, \phi_b = 1.0, \phi_s = 10, n = 4$			
λ	Simulation	Analysis	Error
0.1	7.32 E −3	7.16E −3	2.1%
0.2	1.17E−2	1.15E −2	0.8 %
0.3	1.47E −2	1.45E −2	1.3 %
0.4	1.69E −2	1.68E −2	0.5 %
0.5	1.86E −2	1.87E −2	−0.5 %
0.6	1.99E −2	2.01E −2	−2.0 %
0.7	2.11E −2	2.14E −2	−2.4 %
0.8	2.18E −2	2.24E −2	−2.7 %
0.9	2.26E −2	2.34E −2	−3.5 %
1.0	2.35E −2	2.41E −2	−2.5 %

$\mu = 1, \phi_b = 1.0, \phi_s = 10, n = 5$			
λ	Simulation	Analysis	Error
0.1	7.00E −3	6.77E −3	3.3%
0.2	1.09E −3	1.06E −2	2.7 %
0.3	1.35E −2	1.32E −2	2.2 %
0.4	1.49E −2	1.52E −1	-2.0 %
0.5	1.64E −2	1.67E −2	-2.8 %
0.6	1.79E −2	1.79E −2	0.0 %
0.7	1.91E −2	1.89E −2	1.0 %
0.8	1.97E −2	1.98E −2	−0.5 %
0.9	2.03E −2	2.05E −2	−0.9 %
1.0	2.12E −2	2.12E −2	0.0%

Figure 4.6: Numerical and simulation results for π_{n+1} as a function of load in the DROP Network

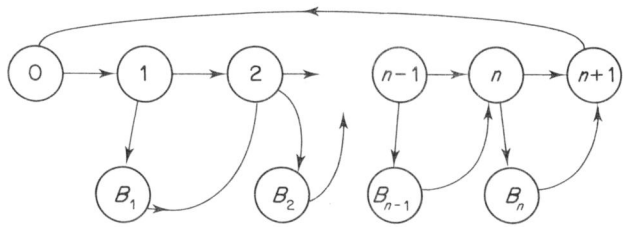

Figure 4.7: State transition diagram of the HOLD network behaviour

where λ_i will be the rate at which transitions occur from state i to state $i+1$ (successful connection) while μ_i will be the rate of transition from state i to state B_i. σ_i will be the rate of transition from B_i to $i+1$ indicating a successful establishment of the connection at level i after being blocked. Let

$$\pi_0, ..., \pi_{n+1}, \pi_{B1}, ..., \pi_{Bn}$$

denote the steady-state probabilities associated with these states. They are linked by the equations

$$\begin{aligned}\lambda\pi_0 &= \phi_s\pi_{n+1} \\ \mu\pi_1 &= \lambda\pi_0 \\ \mu\pi_i &= \lambda_{i-1}\pi_{i-1} + \sigma_{i-1}\pi_{B,i-1}, \qquad 2\leq i \leq n \\ \mu_i\pi_i &= \sigma_i\pi_{Bi}, \qquad 1\leq i \leq n \\ \phi_s\pi_{n+1} &= \lambda_n\pi_n + \sigma_n\pi_{Bn}\end{aligned} \qquad (4.13)$$

where, as in the DROP model, $1/\phi_s$ is the average time it takes to complete a memory access. After some simple manipulations of the above equations we obtain the following equality for $(2 \leq i \leq n)$:

$$\begin{aligned}\mu\pi_i &= \lambda_{i-1}\pi_{i-1} + \sigma_{i-1}\pi_{B,i-1} \\ &= \lambda_{i-1}\pi_{i-1} + \mu_{i-1}\pi_{i-1} = \mu\pi_{i-1}\end{aligned}$$

so that

$$\pi_i = \pi_{i-1}, \qquad 2 \leq i \leq n$$

while

$$\pi_{n+1} = \frac{\mu}{\phi_s}\pi_n$$

and

$$\pi_0 = \frac{\phi_s}{\lambda}\pi_{n+1} = \frac{\mu}{\lambda}\pi_n$$

Thus using

$$\sum_{i=0}^{n+1} \pi_i + \sum_{i=1}^{n} \pi_{Bi} = 1$$

we obtain

$$1 = n\pi_1 + \left(\frac{\mu}{\lambda} + \frac{\mu}{\phi_s}\right)\pi_1 + \pi_1\sum_{i=1}^{n}\frac{\mu_i}{\sigma_i} \qquad (4.14)$$

4.5. The HOLD Network Model

To complete the analysis, we must now derive μ_i and σ_i. This is done via a model for the links as in the previous sections. We represent a link at level i by two states 0_i and F_i (occupied and free, respectively) and denote by $P(0_i)$, $P(F_i)$ their probabilities. Again

$$\mu_i = \mu P(0_i)$$

while τ_i the rate of transition from state 0_i to F_i is the rate ϕ_s of usage of the memory for a processor which is in state $n+1$, given that the processor has already obtained the link of level i, since the end of the memory access will release all links including the level i link. We thus have

$$\tau_i = \frac{\phi_s \pi_{n+1}}{\pi_{n+1} + \sum_{j=i+1}^{n}(\pi_j + \pi_{Bj})} \tag{4.15}$$

The rate σ_i at which a processor obtains a level i link is related to τ_i as follows. Given that the requesting processor has already obtained the $(i-1)$ first links of its access, i.e. given that it is either in state i or B_i, its rate of successful access to the i level link after a failure is simply the rate τ_i at which the link will be freed; thus

$$\begin{aligned}\sigma_i &= \frac{\tau_i \pi_{Bi}}{\pi_{Bi} + \pi_i}, \quad 1 \le i \le n \\ &= \frac{\mu_i \tau_i}{\mu_i + \sigma_i}\end{aligned} \tag{4.16}$$

On the other hand, the rate of transition ε_i from state F_i to 0_i is simply the total request rate

$$\varepsilon_i = \mu \pi_i, \quad 1 \le i \le n$$

since in the HOLD network all requests are guaranteed to be eventually satisfied and assuming that any processor is equally likely to request any path to which it is connected. We then have

$$P(0_i) = \frac{\tau_i}{\varepsilon_i + \tau_i}$$

so that

$$\mu_i = \frac{\mu \tau_i}{\mu \pi_i + \tau_i}, \quad 1 \le i \le n \tag{4.17}$$

The numerical solution of the model can now be obtained using (4.14), (4.15), (4.16), (4.17) which we summarize as follows. Indeed (4.14) yields

$$\pi_1 = \left(n + \frac{\mu}{\lambda} + \frac{\mu}{\phi_s} + \sum_{i=1}^{n} y_i\right)^{-1} \tag{4.18}$$

$\mu = 1, \phi_s = 10, n = 3$			
λ	Simulation	Analysis	Error
0.1	8.76 E −3	8.43E −3	−3.8%
0.2	1.44E −2	1.40E −2	−3.5 %
0.3	1.82E −2	1.76E −2	−3.2 %
0.4	2.06E −2	2.01E −2	−3.5 %
0.5	2.21E −2	2.19E −2	−2.0 %
0.6	2.39E −2	2.33E −2	−3.5 %
0.7	2.47E −2	2.43E −2	−3.5 %
0.8	2.53E −2	2.52E −2	−0.5 %
0.9	2.62E −2	2.59E −2	−2.2 %
1.0	2.61E −2	2.65E −2	1.6%

Figure 4.8: Probability of success π_{n+1} at an output point for a HOLD network

where $y_i = \mu_i/\sigma_i$, while for any given value of π_1 (4.14), (4.15), (4.16), (4.17) will allow us to calculate the y_i. This leads to an iterative algorithm for calculating π_1, and from there for obtaining π_{n+1}.

On Fig. 4.8 we tabulate for a HOLD network with $n = 3$, i.e. with eight processors and as many memory banks, the value of π_4 as a function of the load λ, as obtained using this analysis and a simulation model. The level of accuracy appears again to be particularly good.

4.6 Bibliography

The list of references given below constitute a useful complement to this chapter concerning the performance of interconnection networks.

The networks we have examined here allow the interconnection of 2^n processors with 2^n memory banks, and they include such systems as the Omega [9], Flip [1], Indirect Binary Cube [13], Modified Date Manipulator [6], Baseline and Reverse Baseline [4] systems which have also been discussed in [2, 7, 12].

Performance analysis of multistage networks such as these have been presented in particular with respect to contention in [3,10]. For networks operating in packet switching mode, issues related to resequencing have been examined in [11]; indeed in such systems packets proceeding in the network

4.6. Bibliography

can lose the order in which they have been injected by the time they leave the network, and they must then be reassembled at the output. In [10] Lee and Wu analyse a circuit switching Baseline network both in DROP mode and in the WAIT mode, and they obtain an average value result concerning the transition rates between levels. Patel [12] represents the state of the lines at level i by a Bernoulli random variable whose parameter is obtained via a two-step recurrence relation with the DROP assumption. Dias and Jump [3] study Delta networks operating in packet switching mode with a single buffer at each 2×2 switch. Their model based on representing the network at each memory cycle, assuming that during one cycle packets can move up one level, leads to a very large and intractable Markov chain. They then obtain a simplified approximate model which they solve iteratively.

The approach presented here is inspired by these previous results, but is based on the original work presented in [8] whose main contribution is to improve the accuracy of the analytical evaluation method with respect to previous results.

[1] Batcher, K. E. 'The Flip Network in Staran', *Proc. Int. Conf. Parallel Processing*, pp. 65–71 (August 1976).

[2] Bermond, J.C., Fourneau J. M., and Jean-Marie, A., 'A Graph Theoretical Approach to Equivalence of Multistage Interconnection Networks', Rapport LRI, France (November 1985), to appear in *Discrete Applied Math.*

[3] Dias, D.M. and Jump, J.R. 'Analysis and Simulation of Buffered Delta Networks', *IEEE Trans. on Computers*, Vol. C30, pp. 273–282 (April 1981).

[4] Feng, T. and Wu, C. 'On a Class of Multistage Interconnection Networks', *IEEE Trans. on Computers*, Vol. C29, pp. 694–702 (August 1980).

[5] Feng, T. and Wu, C. Tutorial: 'Interconnection Networks for Parallel and Distributed Processing', *IEEE Publications* (1984).

[6] Feng, T. 'Data Manipulating Functions in Parallel Processors and their Implementations', *IEEE Trans. on Computers*, Vol. C23, pp. 309–318 (March 1974).

[7] Fourneau, J.M. 'Modélisation des Réseaux d'interconnection', *Thèse de troisième cycle*, Univ. Paris-Sud, France (1985).

[8] Fourneau, J.M. and Gelenbe, E. 'Modélisation d'un Réseau Multi-étages', *Actes du Colloque C3 (CNRS)*, Angoulême, France (1987).

[9] Lawrie, D. H. 'Access and Alignment of Data in an A.P.', *IEEE Trans. on Computers*, Vol. C24, pp. 1145–1155 (December 1975).

[10] Lee, M. and Wu, C. L. 'Performance Analysis of Circuit Switching Baseline Interconnection Networks', *Proc. IEEE Symposium on Computer Architecture* (1984).

[11] Mitra, D. and Cieslak, R. 'Randomized Parallel Communications on an Extension of the Omega Network', Bell Labs, Technical Report, Murray Hill, USA (1986).

[12] Patel, J. H. 'Performance of Processor-Memory Interconnections for Multiprocessors', *IEEE Trans. on Computers*, Vol. C30, pp. 771–779 (1981).

[13] Pease, M. C. 'The Indirect Binary Cube Microprocessor Array', *IEEE Trans. on Computers*, Vol. C26, pp.458–473 (May 1977).

5

Parallel Program Performance: Series-Parallel Program Structures

5.1 Introduction

In Chapter 2 we have presented a general discussion of the interaction between program structure and computer architecture in the determination of the performance of parallel computer architectures. The issue was discussed again in the context of simple models in Chapter 3. However even if the multiprocessor systems' architecture were ideal, with an unlimited number of processors accessing an infinite random access memory with no memory conflicts, it would still not be possible to achieve unlimited speed-up using parallel processing. This is simply because, as indicated in Chapter 2, many operations executed by programs require a partial or fully sequential order execution. Thus the order of execution of the primitive tasks in a program is largely responsible for determining the performance of the parallel computer architecture. As indicated in Chapter 2, the order of execution of the primitive tasks is determined by a task graph which represents each individual task in the program and the precedence order between tasks as well as other information which may be of interest, such as the nature and amount of information to be transferred between tasks. Some program control structures can be adequately represented by 'series-parallel' task graphs (SPTG). For instance, the fork-join structures common to certain programs are of this type. However, performance evaluation results are of greater significance if they relate to families of programs, rather than to individual programs unless the latter are of particular importance or significance. Therefore we shall consider the parallel processing performance of families of series-parallel task graphs. Such families will be represented in a compact fashion by a probability model. The model will characterize each family of series-parallel task graphs by three parameters: the average number of tasks in the graph or size of the program, the average execution time of an individual task, and the relative frequency of parallel structures with respect to sequential structures. These three parameters will completely determine the ideal average execution time and average speed-up of the family of programs assuming an unlimited number of processors. In Section 5.2, we present the series-parallel task graph structure and the corresponding model for program families. In Section 5.3, the statistical properties of the random graph representing a particular family of programs is discussed. Section 5.4 is devoted to the presentation of the computational method which is used to derive the distribution of the execution time of programs in the family. We complete the presentation with a numerical result. The method we present in this chapter, like the one presented in the following one (Chapter 6) can be used in practice to determine from a very small number of parameters what the best possible speed-up can be for a family of programs. This information can then be used in many ways. It can be used to choose the appropriate number of processors in a machine architecture which will execute this family of programs; indeed, this number should not be too much larger than the speed-up, since otherwise processing capacity will be wasted. It can also be used to understand the practical speed-up encountered when running the family of programs on a given architecture; for instance if the effective speed-up is much lower than its theoretically expected value and if the number of processors is adequate, then there are other factors in the architecture, such as memory contention or input-output due to insufficient memory, which are limiting performance.

5.2 The SPTG Model of Program Structure

A program whose structure is a SPTG is shown in Fig. 5.1; nodes represent tasks, while arcs represent the precedence relation concerning the execution of the tasks. A task is an indivisible granule of computation; this is the level at which we have, for some appropriate reason, decided to stop refining the program's structure.

5.2. The SPTG Model of Program Structure

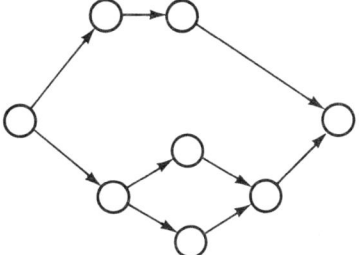

Figure 5.1: SPTG graph

The smallest possible granule is an instruction, if we consider a conventional CPU. If we decompose the internal structure of the CPU into its processing components, then the granularity of a task can be finer than an instruction. Usually, a task shall be a set of instructions which have been grouped together into an indivisible unit which will be executed on a single processor. Obviously, if we are dealing with an array or vector processor, then a task itself may be composed of a set of parallel operations, yet indivisible with respect to the processor being used.

A SPTG can be constructed by successive refinement, starting from an initial node representing the whole program and using the following three simple rules (see Fig. 5.2):

- a node may be replaced by a primitive node or task,

- a node may be replaced by a set of nodes in parallel,

- a node may be replaced by a set of nodes in series.

Obviously, if the first replacement rule is very likely to occur, then the SPTG composed only of tasks will be rapidly created with each node being finally replaced by a task. This process is illustrated in Fig. 5.3. This SPTG generation process using the three replacement rules is quite appealing since it mimics the manner in which a program's designer may structure his code by top-down refinement.

In order to obtain a family of task graphs, we shall introduce some probabilities related to these replacement rules.

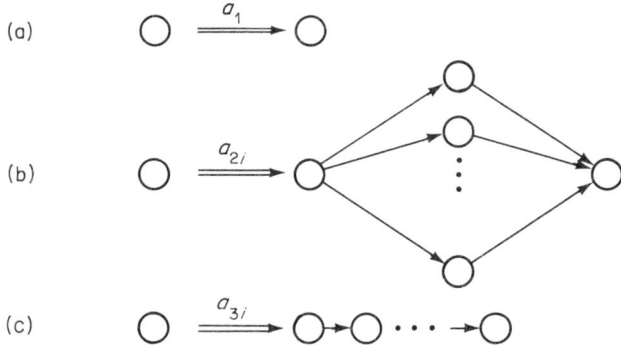

Figure 5.2: Subgraphs for replacement

5.2.1 Stochastic Model for a Family of SPTG

We consider parallel computer programs whose structure is governed by certain stochastic laws. From the laws, a variety of information about the processing requirements of the program is derived, namely

- Properties of the program task graph (the distribution and moments of the number of primitive modules).

- The distribution of the program completion time with an unlimited number of processors.

- The relationship of the mean completion time to the number of processors.

The stochastic laws governing the program structure describe how its graph can be constructed recursively, by successive refinement of its modules.

The recursive construction process is similar to top-down development of a program by successive refinement. It begins by regarding the program as an undefined module, and replacing it by a graph (its replacement) according to a stochastic replacement rule. The parallel or sequential structure of the subgraph is selected according to probabilities which are part of the replacement rule. The subgraph itself contains modules which are further refined by applying the same rule, or a second level rule; one of the possibilities is replacement by a primitive module which contains no parallel execution, and for which the execution-time distribution is known. This replacement process continues until the graph contains only primitive modules.

5.2. The SPTG Model of Program Structure

At any level of the construction process, we select one of the following alternatives by a Bernoulli trial with probabilities $a_1, a_{22}, a_{23}, \ldots, a_{2n}, a_{32}, a_{33}, \ldots, a_{3n}$.

(1) With probability a_1 the subgraph is a simple task or a primitive module (Fig. 5.2a)

(2) With probability a_{2i} ($2 \leq i \leq n$) the subgraph is composed of i modules in parallel (Fig. 5.2b)

(3) With probability a_{3i} ($2 \leq i \leq n$) the subgraph is composed of i modules in series (Fig. 5.2c)

Fig. 5.3 shows three stages in constructing a program in this manner, starting with a single non-primitive module. The final program is identical to the one given in Fig. 5.1. Notice that for simplicity in this study the replacement rules are always the same, and the primitive modules have a common execution-time distribution. As a consequence, every non-primitive module is statistically equivalent. Furthermore, each non-primitive module's execution time is statistically independent of that of the other modules in the generation process.

The probability distribution function of the execution time of a primitive module or task will be given by $F_p(t)$.

In the introduction we had indicated that the model we develop will characterize each family of SPTG by three parameters: the average number M of tasks in a program of the family, the average execution time τ of an individual task, and the relative frequency ϕ of parallel structures with respect to sequential structures. The model which we have presented provides greater detail than these three parameters; however M, τ and ϕ are readily available from the above description.

Indeed, we have simply

$$\tau = \int_0^\infty t \, dF_p(t)$$

Without loss of generality and to simplify the discussion we shall assume that $\tau = 1$ in the sequel. In practice, $F_p(t)$ will be determined by an empirical study of the family of programs at hand, and so will τ. Anticipating on the analysis presented in Section 3, we derive M in the following manner:

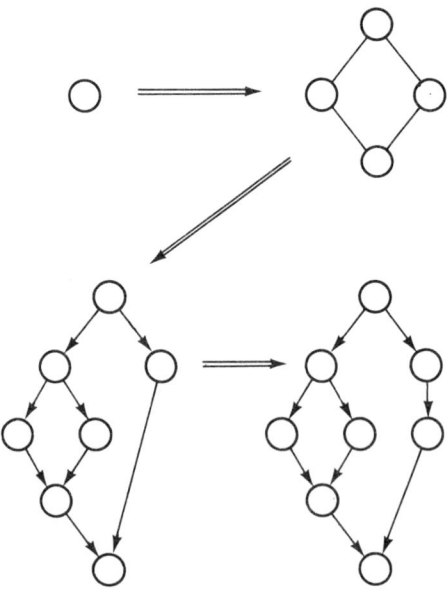

Figure 5.3: The program development process by stepwise refinement

$$M = 1\, a_1 + M \sum_{i=2}^{n} i(a_{2i} + a_{3i})$$
$$= a_1 + M.\gamma$$

where γ is the average number of modules in series or in parallel which may replace a given module. The above equation is derived by noticing that the total average number of tasks in the SPTG is either just 1 if the initial module is replaced by a single task (with probability a_1), or it is equal to the average number γ of modules in series or in parallel by which the initial number module is replaced multiplied by the average number of tasks each such module can generate; the latter quantity is M since each module will generate on the average the same number of tasks as the initial module. We then have simply

$$M = a_1/(1-\gamma)$$

which means in particular that we should have $\gamma < 1$. Obviously, $(a_1, a_{2i}, a_{3i} \geq$

5.2. The SPTG Model of Program Structure

0) for $(i = 2, \ldots, n)$ and

$$a_1 + \sum_{i=1}^{n}(a_{2i} + a_{3i}) = 1$$

So if $a_1 = 1$ we obtain $\gamma = 1$ and $M = 1$: the program is then made of a single task. Consider now an example where $a_{2i} = a_{3i} = 0$ for $(i > 2)$: this is the simplest instance where parallelism or sequential structure of contiguous tasks is allowed. Then

$$\gamma = 2(a_{22} + a_{32}) = 2(1 - a_1)$$

and we have the simple formula

$$M = a_1/(1 - 2(1 - a_1))$$

The parameter ϕ or degree of parallelism is defined as the ratio

$$\phi = \sum_{i=2}^{n} ia_{2i}/\gamma$$

It is an indicator of the average number of subgraphs placed in parallel with respect to the total average number of subgraphs constructed in one step of the refinement procedure for constructing the family of SPTG.

5.2.2 Statistical Properties of the Family of SPTG

In this section we shall develop the statistical properties of the family of task graphs we have introduced above. In particular, we shall derive an expression for the probability distribution of their size, the 'stability' conditions of the graph generation process or the conditions which will guarantee that a finite graph will be generated each time with probability one, as well as other specific properties necessary to the use of the SPTG model.

Let $\alpha_i = a_{2i} + a_{3i}$, $i \geq 1$, and let $\alpha_0 = a_1$. The graph generation process may be viewed as a branching process [7] where α_0 is the probability of extinction. Let N_k denote the number of nodes in the kth generation, where the passage from the kth to the $(k+1)$th generation is defined by the application to each non-terminal node in the kth generation of one of the three (terminal, parallel or series) rules. Clearly

$$N_k = t_k + n_k$$

where t_k is the total number of terminal nodes or tasks up to and including the kth generation and n_k is the number of non-terminal nodes or modules in the k-th generation. We then have

$$P[n_{k+1} = j \mid n_k = i] = P[z_1^k + z_2^k + \ldots + z_i^k = j]$$

where the z_l^k are the number of non-terminal nodes generated by the lth non-terminal node contained in the kth generation. Let $G(x)$ denote the generating function

$$G(x) = \sum_{i=0}^{\infty} \alpha_i x^i \qquad (\alpha_1 = 0)$$

Then

$$P[n_{k+1} = j \mid n_k = i] \equiv [\text{coefficient of } x^j \text{ in } G(x)^i]$$

Let us use the notation:

$$p_k(n) = P[n_k = n]$$

Then

$$p_{k+1}(n) = \sum_{i=0}^{\infty} P[n_{k+1} = n \mid n_k = i] \, p_k(i)$$

where $n_0 = 1$ or $p_0(1) = 1$ is the appropriate initial condition. Hence if we denote by $H_k(x)$ the generating function

$$H_k(x) = \sum_{n=0}^{\infty} p_k(n) x^n \qquad k \geq 0$$

we have the well-known formula [7] for branching processes

$$H_{k+1}(x) = \sum_{i=0}^{\infty} p_k(i) G(x)^i = H_k(G(x))$$

or equivalently

$$H_{k+1}(x) = G(H_k(x))$$

From this formula, we can easily obtain that $E[n_k] = \gamma^k$.

5.2. The SPTG Model of Program Structure

We know that
$$t_{k+1} = t_k + t(n_k)$$
where $t(n_k)$ is the number of *new* terminal nodes in the $(k+1)$th generation. Let $T_k(x)$ denote the generating function

$$T_k(x) = \sum_{n=0}^{\infty} P[t_k = i]x^i$$

Since the number of tasks or terminal nodes added to the $(k+1)$th generation is obtained by choosing at random with probability α_0 whether each non-terminal node or module in the kth generation will be replaced by a task, we have that for any j, $0 \leq j \leq n$:

$$P[t(n_k) = j \mid n_k = n] = \binom{n}{j} \alpha_0^j (1-\alpha_0)^{n-j}$$

and therefore

$$\begin{aligned}\sum_{j=0}^{\infty} P[t(n_k)=j]x^j &= \sum_{n=0}^{\infty}\sum_{j=0}^{\infty} \binom{n}{j} \alpha_0^{n-j}(1-\alpha_0)^j p_k(n) x^j \\ &= \sum_{n=0}^{\infty} p_k(n)[\alpha_0 x + (1-\alpha_0)]^n \\ &= H_k(\alpha_0 x + 1 - \alpha_0)\end{aligned}$$

Therefore, since the generating function of the sum of two independent random variables is the product of their generating functions, we have

$$T_{k+1}(x) = T_k(x) H_k(\alpha_0 x + 1 - \alpha_0)$$

and we obtain the generating function for the distribution of the total number of tasks in the $(k+1)$th generation.

$$T_{k+1}(x) = \prod_{i=1}^{k} H_i(\alpha_0 x + 1 - \alpha_0)$$

Since we already know that $E[n_k] = \gamma^k$, we can compute the average total number of non-terminal nodes generated by this process; it is simply

$$\sum_{0}^{\infty} E[n_k] = 1/(1-\gamma)$$

Obviously, this number will be finite only if $\gamma < 1$. A general recursive formula for $H_k(x)$ has been obtained above. Therefore we can now use the expression for $T_{k+1}(x)$ to calculate the relevant statistics related to t_{k+1}, the number of terminal nodes in the $(k+1)$th generation. In particular, by taking the derivative with respect to x of the expression for $T_{k+1}(x)$ and setting $x = 1$ we obtain, for $u = \alpha_0 x + 1 - \alpha_0$,

$$\begin{aligned} E[t_{k+1}] &= \sum_{i=1}^{k} \alpha_0 \frac{d}{du} H_i(u)\big|_{u=1} \\ &= \alpha_0 \sum_{i=1}^{k} E[n_i] \\ &= \alpha_0 \left(\frac{1 - \gamma^{k+1}}{1 - \gamma} \right) \end{aligned}$$

If we are interested in the average number of tasks or terminal nodes in the SPTG model we take

$$M = \lim_{k \to \infty} E[t_{k+1}] = \alpha_0/(1-\gamma) = a_1/(1-\gamma)$$

5.3 Distribution of Program Execution or Completion Time

Denote by $F(t)$ the distribution function of the execution time t for the program

$$F(t) = P[\text{execution time} \leq t]$$

and by $F_p(t)$ the (known) distribution function of the execution time of a task defined in Section 2.1.

Depending on which replacements occurs, elementary considerations lead the distribution function for a module. For the replacements rules listed in Section 2, we have:

REPLACEMENT	DISTRIBUTION FUNCTION OF EXECUTION TIME
Module	$F(t)$
Task	$F_p(t)$
i modules in parallel	$F^i(t)$ (product of $F(t)$ by itself)
2 modules in series	$F(t) * F(t)$ (convolution) $= \int_0^t \int_0^x f(x-\tau) f(\tau) d\tau dx$
i modules in series	$[F(t)]^{*i}$ (defined to denote i-fold convolution)

5.3. Distribution of Program Execution ...

Indeed, when i modules are placed in parallel, their execution time is the maximum, or if you wish the slowest, of the execution times of each module; if their execution times are independent and identically distributed with distribution function $F(t)$, then the distribution function of the longest execution time will simply be $(F(t))^i$. Similarly, when modules are placed in series the resulting execution times are simply the sum of the individual times, hence the use of the convolution formula.

The distribution function $F(t)$ will denote the distribution of the execution time of a program represented by the SPTG model under the most favourable circumstances: i.e. when the number of processors is unlimited.

Let $S(t)$ denote the probability distribution function (pdf) of the execution time of any module; due to the generation process of 'sub-modules' or sub-programs from any module, $S(t)$ will satisfy the following equation:

$$S(t) = a_1 F_p(t) + \sum_{i=2}^{n} a_{2i}[S_{p1}(t) \cdots S_{pi}(t)]$$
$$+ \sum_{i=2}^{n} a_{3i}[S_{s1}(t) * \cdots * S_{si}(t)]$$

where $F_p(t)$ is the pdf of the execution of a primitive module, while $S_{pj}(t)$ and $S_{sj}(t)$ are, respectively, the pdf of the execution times of the sub-programs placed in parallel and in series. Here the $*$ symbol denotes the convolution of the corresponding density functions.

In fact any $S_{pi}(t)$ or $S_{si}(t)$ will satisfy the same type of equation, so that our model is represented completely by an 'infinite tree' of equations of the same form. Although we shall not provide a formal proof here, it can be established that if a solution exists to this infinite system of equations, then it is in fact the solution $F(t)$ of the following 'fixed point' equation:

$$F(t) = a_1 F_p(t) + \sum_{i=2}^{n} a_{2i}(F(t))^i + \sum_{i=2}^{n} a_{3i}[F(t)]^{*i} \qquad (5.1)$$

This formula relates the execution time of the program to the execution time of the 'sub-programs' which are obtained by step-wise refinement.

5.4 Numerical Solution for the Execution Time Distribution Function

The equation for the distribution $F(t)$ of the execution time derived in the previous section does not have a closed form solution and can therefore only be treated numerically. Indeed, this equation is of interest in its own right and its solution is not a purely routine matter. In this section we shall present a direct algebraic solution approach to obtaining a solution to these equations, and also discuss another approach based on solving a Volterra differential-integral equation.

It is more practical and simple to model execution times as taking discrete values τ_k, say in increments of Δ seconds, $\tau_k = k\Delta$. Let F_k denote $F(\tau_k)$ and F_{pk} denote $F_p(\tau_k)$; then (5.1) becomes

$$F_k = a_1 F_{pk} + \sum_{i=2}^{n} a_{2i} F_k{}^i + \sum_{i=2}^{n} a_{3i} [F]_k^{*i} \qquad (5.2)$$

when discrete-time convolution is used. For $n = 2$ the 2-fold convolution term is

$$[F]_k^{*2} = \sum_{j=0}^{k} (F_j - F_{j-1}) F_{k-j} \qquad (5.3)$$

Note that we set $F_{-1} = F_{-2} = \ldots = 0$. For $n = 2$, (5.2) and (5.3) can be combined and rearranged to give a quadratic equation for F_k, $k \geq 0$:

$$(a_{22} + a_{32}) F_0^2 - F_0 + a_1 F_{p0} = 0 \quad \text{for } k = 0 \qquad (5.4)$$

$$a_{22} F_k^2 + F_k (a_{32} F_0 - 1) + [a_1 F_{pk} + a_{32} \sum_{j=1}^{k} (F_j - F_{j-1}) F_{k-j}] = 0 \qquad (5.5)$$

The solutions of the quadratic equation (5.4) in the interval $[0, 1]$ are given by:

$$F_{0,1} = \frac{1 + \sqrt{1 - 4(a_{22} + a_{32}) a_1 F_{p0}}}{2(a_{22} + a_{32})} \qquad (5.6)$$

$$F_{0,2} = \frac{1 - \sqrt{1 - 4(a_{22} + a_{32}) a_1 F_{p0}}}{2(a_{22} + a_{32})} \qquad (5.7)$$

In order to show that $F_{0,1}, F_{0,2}$ are both non-negative, the expression inside the radical has to be non-negative

$$1 - 4(a_{22} + a_{32}) a_1 F_{p0} \geq 0 \qquad (5.8)$$

5.4. Numerical Solution for the Execution Time ...

As a consequence of the condition $\gamma < 0$ for convergence of the branching process, we must have
$$2(a_{22} + a_{32}) < 1$$
with
$$a_1 + a_{22} + a_{32} = 1$$

Thus (5.7) is positive if and only if $a_1 F_{p0} < \frac{1}{2}$ where, $(0 \le F_{p0} \le 1)$, so both $F_{0,1}$ and $F_{0,2}$ are non-negative. On the other hand, the restriction $(0 \le F(0) \le 1)$, for a distribution function, leads us to determine that $F(0) = F_{0,2}$ is the unique solution.

For $n > 2$ the same approach yields a polynomial equation of order n for F_k, in terms of $F_0, F_1, \ldots, F_{k-1}$. For example, for $k = 0$ (5.2) becomes

$$F_0 = a_1 F_{p0} + \sum_{i=2}^{n} a_{2i} F_0^i + \sum_{i=2}^{n} a_{3i} F_0^i$$

$$F_0 = \sum_{i=2}^{n} (a_{2i} + a_{3i}) F_0^i + a_1 F_0 \qquad (5.9)$$

Let us now return briefly to the continuous time version, $F(t)$ can be determined by solving the following differential equation which is obtained from (5.1)

$$f(t) = a_1 f_p(t) + \sum_{i=2}^{n} i a_{2i} F^{i-1}(t) f(t) + \sum_{i=2}^{n} a_{3i} [f(t)]^{*i} \qquad (5.10)$$

in which we have used

$f(t) = \frac{dF}{dt}$	• the probability density function of the completion time
$[f(t)]^{*i}$	• the i-fold convolution of $f(t)$ with itself
$[f(t)]^{*2} = \int_0^t f(\tau) f(t - \tau) d\tau$	• for $i = 2$ in the convolution
$f_p(t)$	• the density function for the execution time of an individual task

For $n = 2$, equation (5.10) can be written in the form

$$y'(t) = a_1 f_p(t) + 2 a_{22} y(t) y'(t) + a_{32} \int_0^t y'(\tau) y'(t - \tau) d\tau$$

with $y' = f(t)$

This equation is a Volterra ordinary differential equation, and can be integrated numerically by standard methods, although the effort of computing each step increases with the value of t because of the integral on the right-hand side. We shall not pursue this approach any further in the present treatment.

5.4.1 The Computational Algorithm

The solution of the nonlinear equation (5.5) is computed by an iterative method. A multi-point iteration method can be constructed by rewriting (5.5) in the form:

$$a_{22}F_k^2 + F_k(2a_{32}F_0 - 1) + a_{32}\left[-F_{k-1}F_0\sum_{j=1}^{k-1}(F_j - F_{j-1})F_{k-j}\right] + a_1 F_{pk} = 0,$$

for $k > 0$, which has the following solution:

$$F_k = \frac{-\Phi \pm \sqrt{\Phi^2 - 4a_{22}[a_{32}(-F_{k-1}F_0\sum_{j=1}^{k-1}(F_j - F_{j-1})F_{k-j}) + a_1 F_{pk}]}}{2a_{22}} \tag{5.11}$$

where

$$\Phi = (2a_{32}F_0 - 1)$$

Having as its initial condition $F_0 = 0$ and $F_{-1} = 0$, the equation (5.11) suggests the following iterative formula

$$F_k = \frac{1 - \sqrt{4a_{22}[a_1 F_{pk} + a_{32}\sum_{j=1}^{k-1}(F_j - F_{j-1})F_{k-j}]}}{2a_{22}} \tag{5.12}$$

5.4.2 A Numerical Example

As a numerical example, consider the case when the discrete approximation of the probability distribution function of the execution time of a task is assumed to be uniform on the interval $[0, 1]$:

$$F_p(t) = \begin{cases} 0, & \text{if } t \leq 0 \\ t, & \text{if } 0 < t < 1 \\ 1, & \text{if } t \geq 1 \end{cases}$$

5.4. Numerical Solution for the Execution Time ...

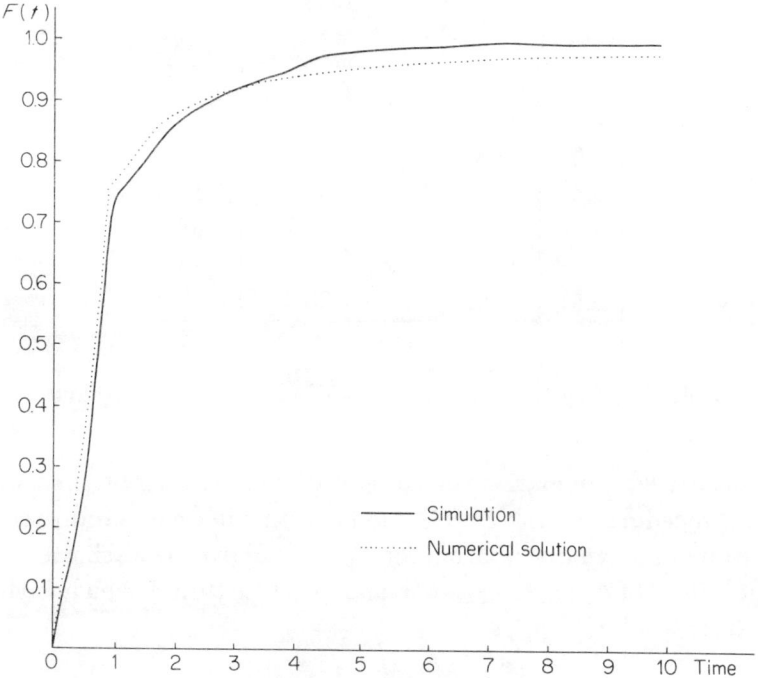

Figure 5.4: Distribution function of program completion times

Equation (5.12) has then been used to compute the numerical approximation to the distribution of program execution time with $\Delta = 0.1$ (the dotted line shown in Figure 5.4) with the following parameter values: $a_1 = 0.51$, $a_{22} = 0.392$, $a_{32} = 0.098$. Since we have (see Section 5.2.1):

$$\tau = 0.5 , \quad \gamma = 0.98$$

we have that the average number of tasks in the program is given by

$$M = a_1/(1 - \gamma) = 25.5$$

so that the average execution time of the program on a single processor would be $M\tau$ or 12.75 time units. The numerical construction of $F(t)$ indicates that the average execution time for this program model with an unlimited number of processors is 3.706 time units, with a speed-up factor of 3.44 with respect to a sequential execution. On Fig. 5.4 we have also plotted a simulation experiment's resulted, conducted with 95% confidence interval, in order to estimate $F(t)$ and to compare it with the numerical results presented on the same figure.

a_1	a_{22}	a_{32}	$M\tau$	S
1	0	0	0.5	1
0.9	0.08	0.02	0.563	1.07
0.8	0.16	0.04	0.67	1.17
0.7	0.24	0.06	0.875	1.38
0.6	0.32	0.08	1.5	1.98
0.51	0.392	0.098	25.5	3.44

Table 5.1: Speed-up factor S for different parallel programs

In Table 5.1 we summarize the computational results obtained with our numerical procedure for the SPTG model with different parameter values with the same uniform distribution for $F_p(t)$ as above. In each case we have shown the values of a_1, a_{22}, a_{32}, $M\tau$ and the speed-up S which is the ratio with $\tau = 0.5$:

$$S = M\tau / \int_0^\infty t\, dF(t)$$

of the average execution time with one processor, to the average execution time with an infinite number of processors.

The speed-up factor shown here can only be predicted using our numerical method, or using more time-consuming simulation experiments. It is interesting to note that it remains moderate which would tend to show that on the average the number of processors used is relatively small.

5.5 Bibliography

Task graphs have been used by several authors to model parallel and sequential activities in parallel programs. The nodes are activities or modules, and a directed arc from one module to another shows that the second requires prior completion of the first. When the module execution times are deterministic, critical path analysis [1] can be used to find the program completion time. When module execution times are stochastic, the probability distribution of the completion time can be determined by a straightforward but in general very costly computation [2, 3].

A study of performance evaluation issues for parallel programs and a model for machine independent evaluation of parallel algorithms can be

5.5. Bibliography

found in [4]. On the other hand, modelling the program behaviour of tree-like programs when an infinite number of processors is available has been considered elsewhere [5,6].

The present chapter is largely based on the model presented in [8].
Other relevant references will be discussed in Chapter 6.

[1] Coffman, E. G. and Denning, P.J. *Operating System Theory*, Prentice-Hall, Englewood Cliffs, N.J. (1973).

[2] Herzog, U. and Hoffmann, W. 'Synchronization Problems in Hierarchically Organized Multiprocessor Computer Systems', in *Performance of Computer Systems*, Proc. 4th Int. Symp. Modeling Performance Evaluation Computer Syst. North-Holland, Amsterdam, pp. 29–48 (1979).

[3] Baker, K. R. *Introduction to Sequencing and Scheduling*, John Wiley & Sons, New York (1974).

[4] Tripathi, S. K. 'On Detecting Parallelism in Software', *ISEM Research Report, No. 31*, Université Paris-Sud, France (1984).

[5] Mussi, P. and Nain, P. 'Evaluation of Parallel Execution of Program Tree Structures', *INRIA Research Report No. 318*, France (1984).

[6] Fayolle, G., King, P. J. B. and Mitrani, I. 'On the Execution of Programs by Many Processors', *Proceedings of 'Performance' 83'*. North-Holland, Amsterdam, pp. 217–228 (1983).

[7] Cox, D. R. and Miller, H. D. *The Theory of Stochastic Processes*, Chapman and Hall, London (1977).

[8] Gelenbe, E., Montagne, E., Suros, R., Woodside, C. M. 'A Performance Model of Block-Structured Parallel Programs', in *Parallel Algorithms and Architectures*, M. Cosnard et al. (ed.), pp. 127–138, North-Holland, Amsterdam (1986).

6

General Acyclic Random Graphs as Models of Parallel Programs

6.1 Introduction

In Chapter 5 we have considered multiprocessing computer systems in which a job is divided into a number of tasks, each executing on a processing unit concurrently with other tasks, with the important assumption that these tasks are structured in series-parallel mode. The division of a program into a set of tasks is governed by its logical structure and by the interdependence among tasks. Such a program structure can be described by a computation or task graph where vertices or nodes represent tasks and directed edges represent precedence relations. The model we consider represents the *execution* of a parallel program rather than its logical structure.

The computation graph or task graph model is characterized by the number of tasks, their processing times, and the structure of the precedence relations. In the previous chapter we have considered series-parallel task graphs which constitute a useful and interesting representation for certain parallel programs. Nevertheless it is clear that all parallel program structures cannot be adequately covered in this manner.

In this chapter we shall consider a class of computation or task graphs having an arbitrary structure. The only constraint will be that each graph of the family must be acyclic; this is most reasonable since if the computation graph of a program contains cycles, then this program will eventually deadlock and will therefore not terminate its execution.

In Sections 6.1 to 6.5 we shall discuss task graphs in which *communication times* between tasks are neglected. In Section 6.6 we analyse the effect of communication times.

The key results in this chapter are Theorem 1 which deals in longest paths in task graphs without communication times, Theorem 3 which generalizes it to the case with communication times, and Theorem 5 which tells us that the best possible computation time for a parallel program (with or without communication times) increases linearly with the number of tasks in the program.

Consider now a program composed of K tasks denoted by $(1, ..., K)$ and for each task i let $\tau(i)$ denote its execution time. A directed graph represents the precedence relations between tasks. Let A denote the incidence matrix of this graph with elements $a(i,j)$ where i and j denote nodes or tasks; $a(i,j) = 1$ will imply that task j cannot begin its execution unless node i has terminated while $a(i,j) = 0$ will mean that there is no direct dependence between i and j. Clearly the graph will be directed; however it will be acyclic since we do not wish to consider programs with deadlocks, i.e. with mutual waits between two or more tasks.

Since the task graph is acyclic, it is isomorphic (identical in structure, up to a renumbering of the nodes) to a graph with the following properties concerning its nodes $(1, ..., K)$:

- node 1 has no predecessors

- node K has no successors

- more generally, $a(i,j) = 0$ for $j < i$.

Thus by renumbering the nodes of the original task graph, we obtain a graph in which arcs (or arrows) go only from smaller numbered nodes to larger numbered nodes. Henceforth we only deal with this type of graph.

We define a *path* in the graph: it is a sequence of nodes $(i_1 < ... < i_l)$ such that

$$\begin{aligned} a(i_j, i_{j+1}) &= 1 \\ a(i, i_1) &= 0 \quad \text{for all } i < i_1 \\ a(i_l, j) &= 0 \quad \text{for all } j > i_l \end{aligned}$$

Thus a path is a set of ordered connected nodes such that its first element has no predecessors and its last element has no successors.

6.1. Introduction

The *length* of the path will be the sum of the execution times of the tasks on the path. Clearly this differs from the usual definition in graph theory where the length of a path is merely the number of nodes on the path. Thus for the path $\pi = (i_1, ..., i_l)$ its length $T(\pi)$ is

$$T(\pi) = \sum_{j=1}^{l} \tau(i_j)$$

A *critical path* $\hat{\pi}$ of the task graph is a longest path, i.e. $\hat{\pi}$ is one of the paths for which $T(\hat{\pi})$ is the greatest among all paths π of the task graph:

$$T(\hat{\pi}) \geq T(\pi) \text{ for all } \pi \text{ in the graph}$$

Clearly :

- different paths are not necessarily disjoint, since they can share tasks or nodes,
- there may be several critical paths, each of course with the same length,
- a critical path may have fewer tasks or nodes than some other path, and yet have a longer execution time including waiting.

A critical path however has a particularly important characteristic; if the program represented by a given task graph is executed with an *unlimited* number of processors, then $T(\hat{\pi})$ will be the corresponding total execution time assuming ideal conditions (unlimited memory, no memory access conflicts, negligible communication time between tasks).

Thus $T(\hat{\pi})$ is the *minimum execution time* of the program or task graph; the execution time will always be at least as large as $T(\hat{\pi})$ when the number of processors is finite rather than unlimited. Furthermore, $T(\hat{\pi})$ can also be used to measure the degree of parallelism in the task graph or program.

Indeed, it is clear that if the program is executed on a *single* processor equivalent to any one of the processors in the multiprocessor system, then, again under ideal conditions, the total execution time will simply be

$$C = \sum_{i=1}^{K} \tau(i)$$

thus

$$S \equiv C/T(\hat{\pi})$$

is the maximum speed-up to be obtained with this task graph.

For a given task graph we shall denote by T the length of a critical path: $T \equiv T(\hat{\pi})$.

In order to better understand the structure of task graphs, consider the following graph decomposition.

From a given task graph G with K nodes we shall construct two task graphs G_1 and G_2 as follows:

- G_1 will contain nodes $(1, ..., N)$
- G_2 will contain nodes $(N+1, ..., K)$

so that G_1 and G_2 are obtained from G by setting in the incidence matrix A of G:

$$a(i,j) = 0 \text{ if } (1 \leq i \leq N, \ N < j \leq K)$$

Thus G_1 and G_2 are obtained by 'tearing apart' nodes $(1, ..., N)$ from nodes $(N+1, ..., K)$.

Let T_1 and T_2 denote the length of the critical paths of G_1 and G_2, respectively.

We shall now establish a simple but an important property of task graphs.

Theorem 1.
$$T \leq T_1 + T_2$$

The Theorem states that the execution time T of a task graph (with an unlimited number of processors) can never exceed the sum of the execution times of any two disjoint subgraphs from which the original graph can be constituted. The result is obvious if $N = K - 1$, i.e. if we are constructing a graph with K tasks by adding a task to a graph with $K - 1$ tasks. In its most general form it is a consequence of the Lemma proved below.

Lemma 1. Consider three vectors u, v, w of real numbers such that

$$u = (u_1, ..., u_n), \quad v = (v_1, ..., v_m), \quad w = (w_1, ..., w_r)$$

with the following property. For each w_i, there exits a u_j and a v_k such that:

- either $w_i = u_j$

6.1. Introduction

- or $w_i = v_k$
- or $w_i = u_j + v_k$

Let

$$\hat{u} = \max[u_1, ..., u_n], \quad \hat{v} = \max[v_1, ..., v_m], \quad \hat{w} = \max[w_1, ..., w_r]$$

Then

$$\hat{w} \leq \hat{u} + \hat{v}$$

Proof: There are three possibilities to be considered, because $\hat{w}$ is an element of the vector w:

- if $\hat{w} = u_{j'}$, for some j', then $\hat{w} \leq \hat{u}$ since $u_{j'} \leq \hat{u}$;
- if $\hat{w} = v_{k'}$, for some k', we have the same argument as above;
- finally if $\hat{w} = u_{j'} + v_{k'}$ for some j', k' it follows that

$$\hat{w} \leq \hat{u} + \hat{v}$$

simply because $u_{j'} \leq \hat{u}$, $v_{k'} \leq \hat{v}$, QED.

The Theorem is a direct consequence of the Lemma. Indeed for the graph G, we constitute the vector w containing the *lengths* $w_1, ..., w_r$ of all of its paths. u and v are the vectors containing the lengths of all paths in G_1 and G_2 respectively. Each path in G is either a path in G_1, or a path in G_2, or it is composed of a path in G_1 followed by (or concatenated with) a path in G_2. Thus each path length w_i of G is either a path length u_j of G_1, or a path length v_k of G_2, or $w_i = u_j + v_k$ for some j, k. Since T, T_1, T_2 are the maximum elements of w, u, v, respectively, the result follows, QED.

Practical and theoretical consequences of the Theorem

From a practical viewpoint, in many cases one is interested in the specification of a task graph from the specification of smaller task graphs. Indeed, a very large parallel program may be constructed by 'sticking together' smaller parallel programs. Theorem 1 states that the best possible execution time of a large parallel program is always *smaller* than the sum of the run-times of the component sub-programs. Therefore we can safely estimate the run-time of the larger program by examining the sub-programs.

A theoretical consequence of the result concerns the convergence of the measure defined by
$$\gamma_K \equiv T_K/K$$
Indeed, this measure is of interest because the average task execution time of a task is defined by
$$\tau \equiv \frac{1}{K} \sum_1^K \tau(i)$$
and T_K determines the maximum speed-up which may be expected from the program, which is
$$S_K \equiv \frac{K\tau}{T_K} = \frac{\tau}{T_K/K} = \tau/\gamma_K$$
or the ratio of the sequential execution time to the parallel execution time; thus, τ may be removed from the expression for S_K since it may be viewed as a constant, and the main quantity of interest is γ_K. The property established in Theorem 1 guarantees that, under some further conditions, γ_K converges to a limit. In Section 6.3 we compute the value of this limit for certain task graph models, while in Section 6.2 we discuss how this limit is obtained.

We shall consider the following special model of task graphs.

6.1.1 A random graph model for a family of programs

The task graph model we have just considered is a representation for the execution of a single parallel program. If we wish to consider the execution of a *family* of programs we have to introduce some statistical information concerning the precedence relations and the execution times.

We now take a probabilistic model where $a(i,j)$ defined above are random variables with
$$\begin{aligned} p &= P[a(i,j) = 1] \quad \text{if } j > i \\ 1 - p &= P[a(i,j) = 0] \quad \text{if } j > i \end{aligned}$$
Also, the $\{a(i,j)\}$ are all independent. We shall also suppose that $\{\tau(i)\}$ are independent random variables having the same distributions; τ will denote the corresponding generic random variable. For the sake of simplicity we take
$$E[\tau] = 1$$

6.1. Introduction

without loss of generality.

Thus we consider a general model of parallel computation given by a random, directed, acyclic graph consisting of K nodes in which an arc from node i, $(i = 1, 2, ..., K-1)$ to node j, $(j = i+1, i+2, ..., K)$ exists with probability p. As in Chapter 5, each node corresponds to a task that is to be processed and each directed arc represents a precedence relationship that must be satisfied during processing. We are dealing here with computation graphs whose size (in number of tasks) is fixed, though this size K can be chosen in an arbitrary fashion. The structure of the graphs is arbitrary, and the density of the precedence relations between tasks is determined by the parameter p.

This model will allow us to represent a family of parallel computation graphs, or if you wish a family of parallel programs during execution, where the precedence dependencies among tasks is arbitrary. Nevertheless, this model is characterized by only three parameters: the size K of the program in terms of the number of tasks it contains, the 'relative frequency of precedences' p, and the average execution time of each task $E[\tau]$ which will be discussed below. Thus the structure of this family of programs is described in a very compact manner, which makes it easy to interpret the results obtained.

We also see that a task graph of this family will contain on the average

$$\sum_{i=1}^{K-1} p(K-i) = p(K-1)K/2$$

arcs. Thus on the average each node will have $p(K-1)/2$ successors and as many predecessors.

When p is very small, we can consider that the computation graph represents a program with 'a lot of parallelism', while if p is close to 1 the program will in fact have to be executed sequentially. In reality, the computation graph will correspond to a nearly sequential execution even for relatively small values of p as seen in the sequel.

Let us now briefly review how the present model relates to real parallel programs. The model represents the manner in which a set of programs will run, or alternatively the manner in which a single program may run with different sets of data. The major constraint is that the number of tasks in the program is fixed, i.e. the parameter K is kept constant. From the total, say C, sequential execution time of the program we can then estimate the average task execution time $E[\tau]$:

$$E[\tau] \cong C/K$$

The important parameter p may be estimated from observations of the program behaviour in several manners, some of which are discussed in Section 6.5; a simple approach is to observe the average number N of successors of a task and then set

$$p \cong 2N/K(K-1)$$

Acyclic random graphs have been examined to some extent in the graph theory literature; however when *times* are associated with the nodes (as is necessary in our case) the models we consider are not within the scope of existing graph theoretical results. Such models have, however, been studied in the context of scheduling theory as indicated in Chapters 3 and 5. In this chapter we shall be interested in the average execution time for this class of task graphs, assuming that the number of processors available is *unlimited*. This means in fact that we are considering the most favourable conditions.

Indeed, the analysis we present in this chapter will allow us to estimate the best speed-up which may be obtained for a family of programs represented by the task graph model. If C is the average time it takes to run a program of this family with a *single* processor, and if $T_K(p)$ denotes the corresponding average time when there are more processors than available tasks, e.g. when the number of processors exceeds K, then the speed-up can never exceed

$$S = C/T_K(p) = KE[\tau]/T_K(p)$$

with any number of processors.

The execution time for the computation graph with an unlimited number of processors is also the 'make-span', or longest path from any source node (i.e. a node with no predecessors) to any sink node (i.e. a node with no successors) for the graph. Of course, the path lengths are the sums of the *execution times* of the *tasks* along the path.

In Section 6.3, we shall derive an expression for $T_K(p)$; this expression will be approximate in the sense that it is only valid when K is very large, in addition to the effect of the particular probability model we consider. In Section 6.4 we shall compare this expression to predictions obtained from a simulation model. The use of this result and problems related to the estimation of p for real programs will be discussed in Section 6.5.

Notice that $T_K(p)$ is the same quantity as the parameter T discussed in Chapter 3 (see for instance Figure 3.1).

6.2 Asymptotic Properties of the Speed-up

In this section we shall consider the asymptotic properties of γ_K in the context of a probability model which is far more general than the model of Section 6.1.1. The key variable to this analysis will be T_K. We shall follow here the approach taken by Vincent [6]. In order to do this we change our notation slightly.

T_K will be denoted $T_{1,K}$, to indicate that task 1 is the first task of the graph whose 'smallest execution time' or 'longest path' is T_K.

More generally we shall denote by $T_{m,n}$ the longest path of the task graph whose first task is task m and whose last task is n, with $(m \leq n)$. We shall imagine that we begin with an infinite (acyclic) task graph, with tasks numbered $(1, 2, ..., K, ...)$ from which we can extract a subgraph beginning at task m and ending at task n. Of course we still have the property that for any $(i > j)$, we have $a(i, j) = 0$.

We shall now treat the set of $\{T_{m,n}\}$ for all $(m \leq n)$, as random variables having the following properties:

(1) $T_{m,n} \leq T_{m,l} + T_{l+1,n}$ for any $(m < l < n)$. This is merely a confirmation of Theorem 1.

(2) $T_{m,n}$ has the same probability distribution as $T_{1,n-m+1}$.

   This means that the smallest execution time depends on the number of tasks in the graph but not on their precise identity. This property will be satisfied *in particular* if all the $\tau(i)$ are independent and identically distributed, and if the $a(i, j)$ depend only on the $(j - i)$.

(3) The average value $E[T_{m,n}] \geq -a(n - m)$ for some constant $(a \geq 0)$.

   The main point of the third condition essentially states that the average length of the longest path of a *finite* task graph is *finite*, and furthermore (quite obviously) that it is larger than a quantity such as $-a(n - m)$.

Conditions (1), (2), (3) characterize a 'sub-additive' stochastic process introduced by Kingman[8]. This leads to the following theorem [6].

Theorem 2. Under conditions (1), (2), (3) the stochastic process $\{T_{n,m}\}$ is said to be 'sub-additive'. As a direct consequence we have that as $K \to \infty$

$$\gamma_K = \frac{T_K}{K} \to \beta \text{ (almost surely)}$$

where β is a (non-negative) constant.

Corollary. From the above result we know that the speed-up S of the family of task graphs is given by

$$S = E[\tau(i)]/\beta$$

if $E[\tau(i)]$, the average execution time of a task, does not depend on i.

Condition (1) is a 'natural' property of task graphs, as indicated in Theorem 1. Condition (3) is very reasonable: in fact $E[T_{m,n}] < \infty$ if $E[\tau(i)] < \infty$; furthermore $E[T_{m,n}] > 0$ in practice. Thus the only 'real' condition is (2).

In general, β is difficult to compute. Some specific results concerning β will be given in Section 6.4, both in terms of an analytical approximation and simulation results.

6.3 Asymptotic Analysis of the Mean Processing Time

In this section we shall derive an expression for the average processing time of a family of task graphs assuming that the number of processors available is unlimited, and hence for the maximum speed-up which may be obtained [4]. In the analysis, we shall assume that the task processing times are exponentially distributed random variables. We shall show in particular that the mean processing time varies almost linearly with K, the slope being given by $2p/(1+p)$, assuming (without loss of generality) that $E[\tau(i)] = 1$.

Thus this section is devoted to the computation of an approximation to the quantity β of Theorem 2, when the task execution times are independent and identically distributed exponential random variables.

Consider a particular realization of a computation graph, and relabel the nodes so as to order them according to their completion times. In this reordering we let K be the last node processed, $K-1$ be the second to last one and so on. Consider the effect of adding one more node to this computation graph so as to turn it into a $(K+1,p)$ graph. Clearly, the

6.3. Asymptotic Analysis of the Mean Processing Time

difference in processing time between this $(K+1, p)$ and the (K, p) graph from which it was derived will depend strongly on the arcs coming into the newly added node. Define e_i ($i = 0, 1, ..., K-1$), to be the event that in the reordered graph, an arc exists from node $K - i$ to the newly added node, but no arc exists between node $K - j$ and it for $j < i$. The event e_i occurs with probability $p(1-p)^{i-1}$. By conditioning on these events the average increase in processing time can be written as

$$E[T_{K+1}(p) - T_K(p)] \cong \sum_{i=0}^{K-1} E[T_{K+1}(p) - T_K(p) \mid e_i] \, p(1-p)^i$$

where the approximate equality follows from the fact that the event in which node $K+1$ has indegree 0 has been neglected.

We now evaluate the average increase in processing time conditioned on e_i. If $i = 0$, then clearly the expected processing time is incremented by 1. For $i > 0$, assume that the intercompletion intervals are exponentially distributed with parameter 1. We then have to find the expectation of the positive difference between an exponentially distributed random variable and one whose distribution is E_i.

Let X be an exponentially distributed random variable with parameter 1, and Y be the sum of i independent exponentials with parameter 1. We assume that X and Y are independent. Their density functions are defined on the non-negative real line by

$$\begin{aligned} f_X(x) &= e^{-x}, & x \geq 0 \\ f_Y(y) &= \frac{y^{i-1} e^{-y}}{(i-1)!}, & y \geq 0 \end{aligned}$$

The density function of their positive difference is given by

$$f_{(X-Y)_+}(z) = \int_0^\infty f_X(x+z) f_Y(x) dx = \frac{e^{-z}}{(i-1)!} \int_0^\infty x^{i-1} e^{-2x} dx = \frac{e^{-z}}{2^i}, \quad z > 0$$

The expectation of the positive difference is given by

$$E[(X-Y)_+] = \int_0^\infty \frac{z e^{-z}}{2^i} dz = 0.5^i$$

It follows that

$$E[T_{K+1}(p) - T_K(p)] = \sum_{i=0}^{K-1} p \left(\frac{q}{2}\right)^i \cong \sum_{i=0}^{\infty} p \left(\frac{q}{2}\right)^i = \frac{2p}{1+p}$$

The expected processing time can now be approximated by

$$T_K(p) = T_N(p) + (K - N) \times 2p/(1+p), \qquad K \geq N \qquad (6.1)$$

where the initial value $T_N(p)$ remains to be determined. It is important to note that for a fixed value of p, this result holds for sufficiently large K. If $p \geq 0.1$, this result is valid for graphs with as few as twenty or thirty nodes. On the other hand, if p is close to 0, K may have to be very large indeed (on the order of a thousand nodes) for it to be valid.

6.4 Comparison of the Approximation with Simulation Results

Let us now compare this approximation to results obtained from simulation. Simulations have been run for values of p ranging from 0.01 to 0.9 and values of K in the range of 25 to 500 [4]. Accurate simulation for larger graphs becomes computationally intractable. For each (K, P) graph the simulation was carried out as follows. A random graph was first generated by creating a $K \times K$ adjacency matrix with each element initially set to 0. Random arcs were added to this graph by replacing each zero in the lower triangular portion of the matrix with a 1 with probability p. The resultant (K, P) graph was then simulated to determine its expected processing time. Confidence intervals were derived using independent replications to obtain a 95 percent confidence level.

The results of this simulation are shown in Fig. 6.1 where we also plot the approximation using equation (6.1). The accuracy of the simulation is shown by the fact that the 95 percent confidence interval widths are approximately the same as the size of the points used to indicate the values obtained from simulation. The value of the offset values in equation (6.1), denoted by $T_N(p)$, is given by the simulated values obtained for $N = 25$ and the corresponding value of p. As shown in Fig. 6.1, the theoretical approximation results compare favourably with the simulation results and they are more accurate for large values of p. For small values of p the approximation seems to underestimate the simulated processing time.

On the same figure we also show simulation results when the task execution times are uniformly distributed. These results, showing a straight line relationship between $T_K(p)$ and K confirm Theorem 2. They also show that β (of Theorem 2) strongly depends on p and on the distribution of $\tau(i)$.

6.5. Estimation of p the Probability of Precedence between Tasks

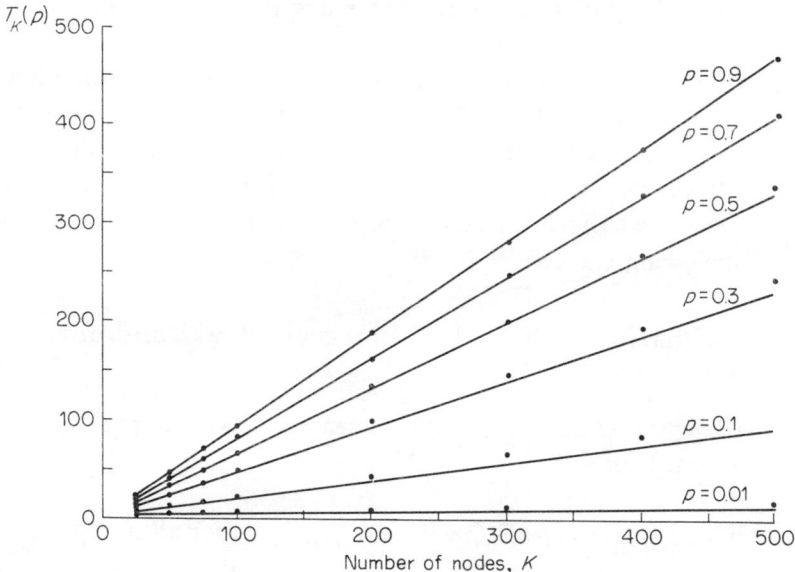

Figure 6.1: Approximate formula for $T_K(p)$ compared with simulation with 95 percent confidence intervals

6.5 Estimation of p the Probability of Precedence between Tasks

From the preceding analysis, and in particular as a consequence of (6.1), the speed-up is then

$$S \cong \frac{KE[\tau]}{E[\tau]T_K(p)} = \frac{1}{\frac{T_N(p)}{K} + (1 - \frac{N}{K})\frac{2p}{1+p}}$$

If K is large and N is much smaller than K, we have

$$S \cong \frac{1+p}{2p} \qquad (6.2)$$

since $T_N(p)$ will be bounded by N in general.

With respect to the analysis presented in Chapter 3, S is also the average number of tasks which are simultaneously active in the same parallel program. Thus if we know S, we can estimate the number of processors which the program actually needs since this number will not exceed S in practice by more then a small multiple.

In order to determine S we need to know p, and this information may not be always readily available.

It may be possible however to estimate p by observing a portion of the program's behaviour. In the following, three approaches to estimate p are presented. The first estimates p from the indegree of a randomly chosen node, the second estimates p from the number of 'roots' or nodes of indegree 0 in the graph, and the third estimates p from the total number of arcs in the graph following the results in [4].

6.5.1 Estimating p from the Indegree of a Randomly Chosen Node

Given the indegree D of a randomly chosen node, we call $\hat{p}(D)$ a *maximum likelihood estimate* of p if

$$P[D \text{ with } p = \hat{p}] \geq P[D \text{ with } p = p'], \qquad \text{for all } p' \in [0,1]$$

Define the likelihood function to be

$$L_K(D,p) = P[\text{Indegree of a randomly selected node} = D]$$

This becomes

$$L_K(D,p) = \frac{1}{(K-D)} \sum_{i=D+1}^{K} \binom{i-1}{D} p^D (1-p)^{(i-D-1)}$$

$$= \frac{1}{(K-D)} \sum_{i=0}^{K-D-1} \binom{D+i}{D} p^D (1-p)^i$$

The ith term in the summation is the probability that node $D+i$ has indegree D multiplied by the number of nodes that can have indegree D. Clearly, this multiplication by a constant cannot affect our answer. Expanding the binomial coefficient out we get

$$L_K(D,p) = \frac{(-p)^D}{(K-D)D!} \frac{d^D}{dp^D} [\sum_{i=0}^{K-D-1} (1-p)^{D+i}]$$

$$= \frac{(-p)^D}{(K-D)D!} \frac{d^D}{dp^D} \sum_{i=1}^{K} \left[\binom{K}{i} - \binom{D}{i}\right] (-1)^{i-1} p^{i-D-1}$$

6.5. Estimation of p the Probability of Precedence between Tasks

Only powers of p greater than D remain after we take the derivative, and we obtain

$$\begin{aligned} L_K(D,p) &= \frac{-1}{K-D}\binom{K}{D} p^{D-1} \sum_{i=0}^{K-D} \binom{K-D}{i} \frac{i}{i+D}(-p)^i \\ &= \frac{-1}{K-D}\binom{K}{D} p^{D-1} \int_0^1 \frac{d}{dx} \sum_{i=0}^{K-D} \binom{K-D}{i}(-x)^i y^{D+i-1}\big|_{x=p} dy \\ &= \binom{K}{D} p^D \int_0^1 y^D (1-py)^{K-D-1} dy \\ &\cong \binom{K}{D} p^D \int_0^1 y^D e^{-pyK} dy \\ &= \binom{K}{D} p^D \frac{D!}{(pK)^{D+1}} \left[1 - e^{-pK} \sum_{i=0}^D \frac{(Kp)^i}{K!} \right] \end{aligned}$$

To find $\hat{p}$ this expression must be maximized, and this is most easily done by differentiating it with respect to p, equating it to 0, and then solving for $\hat{p}$. On doing so, we obtain

$$\frac{(K\hat{p})^{D+1}}{D!} = \sum_{i=D+1}^{\infty} \frac{(K\hat{p})^i}{i!}$$

or

$$\sum_{i=D+2}^{\infty} \frac{(K\hat{p})^{i-D-1} \times (D+1)!}{i!} = D \tag{6.3}$$

If we replace the product $K\hat{p}$ by the single variable x the left side can be seen to be a polynomial of infinite degree. As it is strictly convex, and takes on a value of when $x = 0$, we may conclude that a unique solution exists. This in turn implies that $\hat{p} = \alpha(D)/K$ where $\alpha(D)$ is the solution to the above equation. To ensure numerical stability of the solution to equation (6.3), it is convenient to define the following set of functions: We let $F_0(x) = x/(D+2)$, and let $F_{j+1}(x) = F_j(x)(1 + x/(D+j+3))$. It is clear that $F_j(x)$ is the value of the summation of equation (6.3) truncated at $j + D + 2$. Using these relationships, the equation $F_j(x) - D = 0$ can be approximated numerically to any degree of desired precision by choosing j suitably large. Clearly, p can be estimated from the outdegree of a randomly chosen node in exactly the same manner.

6.5.2 Estimating p from the Number of Roots of the Task Graph

The program's execution begins with the execution of tasks which have no predecessors; in this section we estimate p by observing the number of such tasks.

Let R be the number of roots, or nodes of indegree 0 in a particular realization of a (K,p) graph. As all of these nodes can be processed simultaneously the number of roots in a (K,p) graph is the maximum level of parallelism which can be achieved when the program begins execution. As before, define $\hat{p}(R)$ to be a *maximum likelihood* estimate of p if

$$P[R \text{ with } p = \hat{p}] \geq P[R \text{ with } p = p'], \quad \text{for all } p' \in [0,1]$$

If we define $P_j(K,p)$ to be the probability that a (K,p) graph possesses exactly j roots, the following recurrence can be written for the distribution of the number of roots:

$$P_j(K,p) = \sum_{i=\max[1,j-1]}^{K-1} \binom{i}{i-j+1} p^{i-j+1}(1-p)^{j-1} P_i(K-1,p) \quad (6.4)$$

The ith term in the sum is the probability that the addition of a single node to a $(K-1,p)$ graph with i roots results in a (K,p) graph with j roots. Unfortunately, this recurrence cannot be solved to give $P_j(K,p)$ in closed form, though it can be computed from (6.4) starting with $P_1(1,p) = 1$ and $P_0(1,p) = 0$. On the other hand, the mean of the distribution can be easily found. Define a set of K indicator random variables $\{x_i\}$ as follows:

$$x_i = \begin{cases} 1 & \text{if node i is a root} \\ 0 & \text{if node i is not a root} \end{cases}$$

Clearly, $P[x_i = 1] = (1-p)^{i-1}$. Let X be a random variable that counts the number of roots. Then

$$X = \sum_{i=1}^{K} x_i, \quad \text{and} \quad \bar{X} = \sum_{i=1}^{K} (1-p)^{i-1} = \frac{1 - (1-p)^{K+1}}{p}$$

This leads us to consider the following estimator for p, which is **not** a maximum likelihood estimator. This estimator $\tilde{p}$, is the solution to the equation

$$\tilde{p} = \frac{1 - (1-\tilde{p})^{K+1}}{R} \quad (6.5)$$

6.5. Estimation of p the Probability of Precedence between Tasks

where R is the observed number of roots. Because the distribution of $\tilde{p}$ is unknown, the mean and variance of the estimator cannot be found. Simulation experience with (6.5) indicates that in many cases $\tilde{p}$ is within 5 percent of the maximum likelihood estimate of p [4].

6.5.3 Estimating p from the Number of Edges in the Graph

An obvious approach to estimate p is to count the total number of arcs, when one or more examples of a (K,p) graph are available.

Let α be the number of arcs in a particular sample realization of the graph, and $L_K(\alpha,p)$ be the likelihood function for p. Then, we have

$$L_K(\alpha,p) = \left[\binom{K}{2}\right]_\alpha p^\alpha (1-p)^{\binom{K}{2}-\alpha}$$

If we differentiate this expression and equate it to 0, we find that the maximum likelihood estimate of p, $\hat{p}$ is the solution to the equation

$$\alpha(1-\hat{p}) = \hat{p}\left[\binom{K}{2} - \alpha\right]$$

or that

$$\hat{p} = \frac{\alpha}{\binom{K}{2}}$$

as one would expect from intuitive considerations.

6.6 Task Graphs with Communication Times between Tasks

The task graph model considered in the previous sections does not take into account the effect of communication times between tasks. In this section we generalize the model used to evaluate parallel programs so that when a task i finishes its execution, some other task j such that $a(i,j) = 1$ cannot begin execution unless it receives a message from i and this message takes a time $m(i,j)$ to reach j.

The model we now consider is composed of:

- an infinite set of tasks $(1, ..., K, ...)$ whose execution times $(\tau(1), ..., \tau(K), ...)$ are given,

- a *precedence matrix* $A = (a(i,j))$ such that $a(i,j) = 1$ if i is a predecessor of j, with $a(i,j) = 0$ whenever $j < i$ so that we deal with acyclic task graphs,

- a *message time matrix* $M = (m(i,j))$ where $m(i,j) \geq 0$ whenever $a(i,j) = 1$; $m(i,j)$ will then represent the time necessary to transmit the message indicating to j that i has finished its execution. Clearly, this message can also include data or parameters which i passes to j. if $a(i,j) = 0$ we shall set $m(i,j) = 0$ since it has no effect.

We shall now consider the 'ideal execution time' or minimum execution time t_K of this new model as follows. For any task j first define recursively:

- $t(1) = \tau(1)$
- $t(j) = \tau(j) + \max_{i<j,\ a(i,j)=1}[m(i,j) + t(i)]$

$t(j)$ is obviously the date at which task j will finish its execution given that task 1 begins its execution at time 0. Then we define $\hat{t}$ as :

$$\hat{t} = \max_{1 \leq i \leq K}[t(i) + \max_{j > i}[m(i,j)]]$$

which is the date when the task graph finishes its execution, including the time spent in communication.

This time $\hat{t}$ provides an 'ideal' measure of performance for this task graph since it corresponds to a practical program execution time under the following conditions:

- there is an unlimited number of processors
- there is no contention or queueing at the communication medium (local network, bus, or interconnection network) used to exchange messages between tasks.

Suppose that we now decompose this particular graph with nodes $(1, ..., K)$ into two disjoint subgraphs

6.6. Task Graphs with Communication Times ...

- G_1 with nodes $(1, ..., l)$
- G_2 with nodes $(l+1, ..., K, ...)$

by setting $a(i,j) = 0$ whenever node i is in G_1 $(1 \leq i \leq l)$ and node j is in G_2 $(l+1 \leq j \leq K)$. Obviously no messages will be exchanged between G_1 and G_2.

For each task i let $m(i)$ be the longest communication time associated with its messages

$$m(i) = \sup_{j>i}[m(i,j)]$$

For the task graph, let us now define for each i

$$t'(i) = t(i) + m(i),$$

which is the instant at which task i has finished execution and its messages have been sent, and let the vector t'_k be

$$t' = (t'(1), ..., t'(K)) \qquad (6.6)$$

and

$$\hat{t} = \max_{1 \leq i \leq K}[t'(i)]$$

Thus if we truncate the infinite task graph by keeping only the first K nodes, $\hat{t}$ will be the instant at which it will effectively terminate execution and communication.

Let us now decompose the graph composed of tasks 1 to K into two disjoint graphs

- G_1 including $(1, ..., l)$
- G_2 including $(l+1, ..., K)$

For the tasks of G_1, the corresponding completion times denoted by $t''(i)$ are the same as in G:

$$t'' = t'(i), \qquad 1 \leq i \leq l$$

However for the tasks in G_2, the completion times are different if it is executed in in isolation; we first define

$$\begin{aligned} y(l+1) &= \tau(l+1) \\ y(i) &= \tau(i) + \max_{l+1 \leq j < i}[y(j) + m(j,i)], \qquad \text{for} \quad l+1 \leq i \leq K \end{aligned}$$

and calculate the new completion times as

$$t''(i) = y(i) + m(i), \qquad l+1 \leq i \leq K$$

Let us now introduce the following vectors:

$$\begin{aligned} t_1 &= (t''(1), ..., t''(l)) \\ t_2 &= (t''(l+1), ..., t''(K)) \end{aligned}$$

We now have the following property, which extends Theorem 1 to task graphs with communication times.

Theorem 3.
$$\hat{t} \leq \hat{t}_1 + \hat{t}_2$$

Proof. Indeed each element of the vector t' given in (7.6) is either identical to some element of t_1 or t_2 or, if it is neither of these two, it is no greater than the sum of an element of t_1 and an element of t_2. $\hat{t}$, the largest element of t', will also have this property. Hence the result.

6.6.1 Asymptotic properties of task graphs with communication times

Consider the quantity $\hat{t}$ defined above, which is the instant at which the task graph with a potentially infinite number of tasks has completed its execution and message sending for the first K tasks. We shall henceforth call this quantity T'_K to distinguish it from T_K which does not include communication times.

Let us first state the following obvious result, which does not require proof.

Theorem 4. If $T'_{K+1} < T'_K + T'_K/K$, then there exists an $\alpha \geq 0$ such that

$$\lim_{K \to \infty} \frac{T'_K}{K} = \alpha$$

Now consider the quantity T'_K in a very general framework. We shall construct a random process $\{T'_{n,k}\}$ as follows:

$$T'_{1,k} \equiv T'_k \text{ for all } k \geq 1$$

6.7. Bibliography

on Measurement and Modeling of Computer Systems, pp. 78–87, Cambridge, Mass., USA (August 1984).

[4] Gelenbe, E., Nelson, R., Philips, T. and Tantawi, A. 'The Asymptotic Processing Time for a Model of Parallel Computation', *Proceedings of the National Computer Conference*, Las Vegas, USA (November 1986).

[5] Tsitsiklis, J. N., Papadimitrou, C.H. and Humblet, P.' The Performance of a Precedence-Based Queueing Discipline', *J. ACM*, Vol. 33, No. 3, pp. 593–602 (July 1986).

[6] Vincent, J.M. 'Stability of Precedence-Based Queueing Discipline and Parallel Programs', to appear.

[7] Baccelli, F. and Liu, Z. 'On the Stability Condition of a Precedence-Based Queueing Discipline', to appear in *Advanced Appl. Prob.*

[8] Kingman, J.F.C. 'Subadditive Ergodic Theory', *The Annals of Probability*, Vol. 1, No. 6, pp. 883–909 (1973).

7

Multiprocessor Performance with Task-Graph Models

7.1 Introduction

In the preceding chapters we have seen that the potential for parallelism is often limited by precedence relations within programs and by the finite number of resources in parallel processing systems. Performance predictions for concurrent programs on multiprocessor systems are therefore of crucial importance for both software and hardware designers. Nevertheless not much theory is available for analysing the performance of concurrent programs which have general directed acyclic graph structures and execute on multiprocessor systems with a limited number of processors.

In this chapter, we shall consider the expected response time of concurrent programs executed on multiprocessor systems with a finite number of processors. We use several approximate models to estimate this performance measure.

The multiprocessor system under consideration consists of a finite number of homogeneous processors which share a central memory. Arriving jobs (i.e. concurrent programs) consist of tasks with possibly different execution time distributions. The concurrency and precedence relationship between tasks are defined by directed acyclic graphs of general structure. The arrival of jobs are assumed to be generated by a Poisson process.

Because of the concurrency, the queueing network resulting from such a system does not have a product-form solution. An approximate solution method which models the system by a set of waiting queues for tasks whose predecessors have not yet terminated their execution, and a central server with variable service rate is presented. Some simplifying assumptions are made to derive the estimates of the response time of jobs. The accuracy of the approximation is evaluated through comparisons against simulation results. Some arguments are provided to indicate that these approximations are lower bounds to the expected response time of jobs.

In Section 7.2, we describe the problem in detail. In Section 7.3, the approximate solution when all tasks are statistically identical is described, whereas in Section 7.4, approximate solutions results are compared to simulation results. Section 7.5 provides a method for the case where the workload consists of concurrent programs of different structures.

7.2 The Multiprocessor System Model

We assume that the multiprocessor system under consideration has M identical processors. A main memory is shared by all processors. It is assumed that this memory is of unlimited size so that it can store the address space of all programs which are present in the system. The workload consists of a set of structurally identical concurrent programs consisting of a fixed number of interdependent tasks. The precedence constraints between tasks are defined by an acyclic precedence graph in which each node represents a task.

We consider a stream of jobs (i.e. concurrent programs) arriving to the system according to a Poisson process with parameter λ. All the jobs have the same precedence graph, denoted by G. Assume for the time being that each task requires an exponentially distributed processing time with parameter μ. Processing times of different tasks are assumed to be independent. Let N be the maximum number of predecessors that tasks of graph G may have, $(N \leq m - 1)$, where m is the number of tasks in the job (or nodes in G).

Upon arrival, a job is immediately split into its constituent tasks so that tasks which have no predecessors are ready for immediate execution and enter directly into the processor queue waiting for service by one of the processors. The other tasks, which are not yet available for execution because of precedence constraints, have to wait in a buffer until their predecessors have been serviced.

We model this wait as follows. Tasks having i $(i = 1, 2, \ldots, N)$ predecessors enter buffer i, and wait for their i predecessors' service completion. When the execution of a task is completed (by one of the processors), it

6.6. Task Graphs with Communication Times ...

and more generally we define for all $n \geq 1$:

$$y_{n,n} = \tau(n)$$

and for $k \geq n$:

$$y_{n,k+1} = \tau(k+1) + \sup_{n \leq i \leq k,\ a(i,k)=1} [y_{n,i} + m(i, k+1)]$$

We then take for

$$T'_{n,k} = y_{n,k} + m(k)$$

where we recall that

$$m(k) = \sup_{j > k}[m(k, j)]$$

As in Section 6.2, we construct a sub-additive process $\{T'_{n,k}\}$, ($n \geq 1$, $k \geq n$) with the following properties:

(1) $T'_{n,k} \leq T'_{n,l} +' T'_{l+1,k}$ for any $(n < l < k)$, which is a consequence of Theorem 3.

(2) $T'_{n,k}$ has the same probability distribution as $T'_{1,k-n+1}$, for all $(n \geq 1,\ k \geq n)$; this is the only 'real' restriction on the model.

(3) $E[T'_{n,k}] < \infty$ for all $(k \geq n \geq 1)$, and also $E[t'_{n,k}] \geq -a(k-n)$ for some constant $(a \geq 0)$.

We can now use Kingman's theorem [8] to state

Theorem 5. Let $\gamma'_k = t'_{1,k}/k$. Then there exists $\gamma \geq 0$ such that

$$\lim_{k \to \infty} \gamma'_k = \gamma \quad \text{almost surely}$$

6.6.2 A simulation example of asymptotic speed-up with communication times

The results presented in Section 6.6.1 and more particularly Theorem 5 allows us to estimate the asymptotic speed-up of a parallel program with communication times. Suppose that we have a very large parallel program, i.e. one for which the number K of tasks is very large, its total execution time on a conventional single processor will be

$$C_K = \tau(1) + ... + \tau(K)$$

if we assume that all tasks share the same memory so that the communication times between tasks can be neglected. The speed-up with an unlimited number of processors, but with communication times, will then be

$$S' = \frac{C_K}{T'_K} = \frac{C_K/K}{T'_K/K}$$

If the limit result in Theorem 5 can be used, then S will have the following form:

$$S' \equiv \frac{\text{Average task execution time}}{\gamma}$$

Thus γ is of interest; however it appears very difficult in general to obtain γ in the form of a mathematical expression.

On Fig. 6.2 we represent some simulation results for S', assuming that the average task execution time is 1 in order to simplify the presentation. We provide four curves:

- T'_K as a function of K, when task execution times are exponentially distributed, and so are the communication times which are also of average value 1.

- $T_K(p)$ of Section 6.1 both for exponentially distributed and uniformly distributed task execution times.

- Finally the theoretical curve $T_K(p) \cong 2pK/(1 + p)$ for exponentially distributed task execution times.

All these curves are given for the random task graph model with the same value of p.

6.6. Task Graphs with Communication Times ...

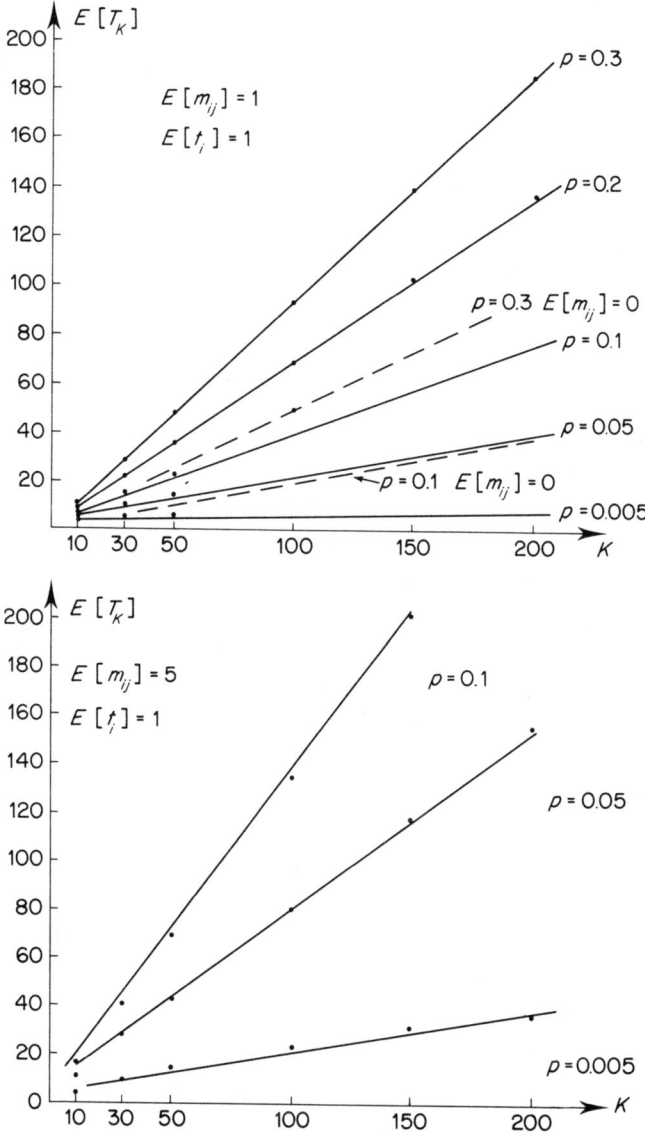

Figure 6.2: Average execution time (simulation results) of the task-graph model with and without communication times

We clearly see that both the distribution of the task execution times and the communication times have a very strong influence on the execution times. We should notice that even though the simulations presented above yield the average values of T_K and T'_K, the slope of the curves in Figures 6.1 and 6.2 are in fact an estimate of T_K/K and T'_K/K as a consequence of the almost sure convergence indicated in Theorems 4 and 5.

6.7 Bibliography

Computation graphs have been examined by several authors as models of parallel processing. Fayolle et al. [1] consider a tree structure where the number of sons of a node in the tree is described by a random variable. They analyse such a structure and obtain the distribution of the total execution time of a job on an infinite number of processors, in the special case that the number of sons is geometrically distributed and the task execution times are constant. Otherwise, numerical solutions are calculated.

Mussi and Nain [3] examine a tree structure with exponentially distributed task processing times and consider two execution policies: (1) level by level and (2) take a leaf. They obtain the Laplace–Stieltjes transform of the total execution time of the tree under the two policies. For policy (1), they assume an arbitrary number of processors. Whereas for policy (2), they assume equal mean task processing times and consider two cases: two processors and an infinite number of processors.

A random graph model of transaction processing systems is considered by Franaszek and Robinson [2]. A node in such a graph represents a transaction and an edge represents a conflict. An edge between pairs of transactions exists with some fixed probability. They obtain bounds on the expected number of transactions that can run concurrently.

The approach developed in this chapter is essentially based on [4], though Theorem 1 and the material in Section 6.6 is new.

[1] Fayolle, G., King, P. J. B., and Mitrani, I. 'On the Execution of Programs by Many Processors', *Proceedings of Performance 88*, North-Holland Publishing Co., Amsterdam, pp. 217–228 (1983).

[2] Franaszek, P. and Robinson, J. T. 'Limitations of Concurrency in Transaction Processing', *ACM Transactions on Database Systems*, Vol. 10, pp. 1–28 (March 1985).

[3] Mussi, P and Nain, J. T. 'Evaluation of Parallel Execution of Program Tree Structures', *Proceedings of the ACM SIGMETRICS Conference*

7.2. The Multiprocessor System Model

leaves the system and may free some tasks waiting in one of the buffers. Once released by all its serviced predecessor tasks, a task leaves the buffer to join the server queue. An arriving job remains active in the system until all of its tasks have completed execution.

7.2.1 The General System Model

An exact representation of the system could be the following. The state of the system is a collection of tasks which are either waiting in a buffer for their predecessor tasks to be terminated, or waiting in queue, or being processed by one of the processors. For a task to be waiting in queue or to be processed, all of its predecessor tasks must be processed. Assuming FIFO service at the processors, the state must also represent the order of arrival of tasks, which is determined by the order in which the programs they belong to have arrived.

Each task will be denoted by a pair of integers (u,v) where u is the program number and v is the task number within the program. The state of the system will be represented by

$$S \equiv (Q, W)$$

where Q and W are defined as follows:

$$Q \equiv \begin{cases} (t_1, t_2, \ldots, t_{|Q|}), & t_i \ (1 \leq i \leq |Q|) \text{ is a task, and we denote by } |Q| \\ & \text{the number of tasks running or ready to run,} \\ \emptyset, & \text{if there are no tasks in the system} \end{cases}$$

The tasks t_l in Q are given in FIFO order with t_1 being at the head of the queue. Therefore the first M of these tasks will actually be running.

$$W \equiv \begin{cases} \emptyset, & \text{if no tasks are waiting} \\ (w_1, w_2, \ldots, w_{|W|}), & \text{if there are } |W| \text{ tasks waiting,} \end{cases}$$

where each w_l is a pair

$$w_l \equiv \{T_l, A_l\}$$

in which T_l is a task and A_l is the set of tasks which are the immediate predecessors of T_l. In fact, A_l will be unnecessary if all the programs running in the system have exactly the same precedence graph; in that particular case the task T_l uniquely identifies the set A_l for all programs. However if programs can have different task graphs, the set A_l will have to be specified.

The analysis of this general state-space model seems beyond the possibilities offered by exact analytical modelling. In order to illustrate the complexity of the model consider the state transition associated with the arrival of a program, from $S = (Q, W)$ to $S' = (Q', W')$:

$$Q' \equiv (t_1, \ldots, t_{|Q|}, t'_{|Q|+1}, \ldots, t'_{|Q|+j}), \quad \text{if there are } j \text{ tasks without predecessors in the arriving program}$$

$$W' \equiv \begin{cases} (w_1, \ldots, w_{|W|}, w_{|W|+1}, \ldots, w_{|W|+k}), & \text{if there are } k \text{ tasks with predecessors in the arriving program} \\ \emptyset, & \text{if } |W| = 0 \text{ and } k = 0. \end{cases}$$

Obviously $w'_l = \{T'_l, A'_l\}$, so that the set of tasks of the arriving program is given by

$$\{T'_{|W|+1}, \ldots, T'_{|W|+k}, t'_{|Q|+1}, \ldots, t'_{|Q|+j}\}.$$

Furthermore the order in which the tasks t'_i which have no predecessors are placed in the processor queue Q' is of importance; we shall assume that they are placed in the order of increasing task number, so that the task with no predecessors and with the smallest task number is placed closest to the head of the queue. This will be the rule which will be used in general for placing tasks in the processor queue.

The representation of the other transactions related to task departures is even more complex. That is why in the rest of this chapter we shall deal with a simplified model in which tasks and their predecessors will not be identified individually, and certain simplifying assumptions will be made about the state transitions.

7.2.2 The Simplified Model

In the simplified model the state of the system will be represented by the vector

$$\mathbf{k} = (k_0, k_1, \ldots, k_N)$$

where k_i is the number of tasks in the system which have i ($1 \leq i \leq N$) predecessors. Recall that N is the maximum number of predecessors which a task may have. k_0 denotes the number of tasks which have no unfinished predecessors at the instant considered. This state representation is obviously much simpler than the general one. However it does not capture in a precise

7.2. The Multiprocessor System Model

manner the structure of the task graph. The transitions from some state **k** to a state **k'** are given as follows for the simplified model.

- The arrival of a program or job represented by a sequence of task arrivals:

    Let λ be the arrival rate of programs to the system. We shall consider a Poisson arrival of tasks of rate λm, m being the total number of tasks per program. Thus we are modelling job arrivals by a flow of single tasks arrivals. Let m_i be the number (or average number for a random program graph) of tasks having i predecessors. Upon arrival of a task,
    $$\mathbf{k} = (k_0, \ldots, k_i + 1, \ldots, k_N), \qquad 0 \le i \le N$$
    with probability chosen to be $p_i \equiv m_i/m$. Notice that $\sum_{i=0}^{N} m_i = m$. The rate of transition from **k** to this particular **k'** is thus $\lambda m p_i$.

- The departure of a task from one of the wait buffers:

    We assume that transitions from state **k** to some state
    $$\mathbf{k'} = (k_0 + 1, \ldots, k_i - 1, \ldots, k_N), \qquad 1 \le i \le N$$
    where $k_i > 0$, occur with rate $\mu_i(k_i)$. These represent the departure rate of a task from the wait buffer into the processor queue. $\mu_i(k_i)$ will be determined as a function of model parameters as given below.

- The departure of a task from the processor queue:

    This will lead into the state
    $$\mathbf{k'} = (k_0 - 1, k_1, \ldots, k_N), \qquad k_0 > 0$$
    with rate
    $$\mu_0(k_0) = \begin{cases} k_0 \mu, & \text{if } 1 \le k_0 \le M \\ M \mu, & \text{if } k_0 > M \end{cases} \qquad (7.1)$$
    Thus we are assuming that all individual tasks have independent exponentially distributed execution times of average value $1/\mu$. We may take $\mu = 1$ without loss of generality.

No other state transitions, except for those given above, are allowed to occur. Fig. 7.1 illustrates the simplified model. In the sequel let $k = \sum_0^N k_i$ denote the total number of tasks in the system.

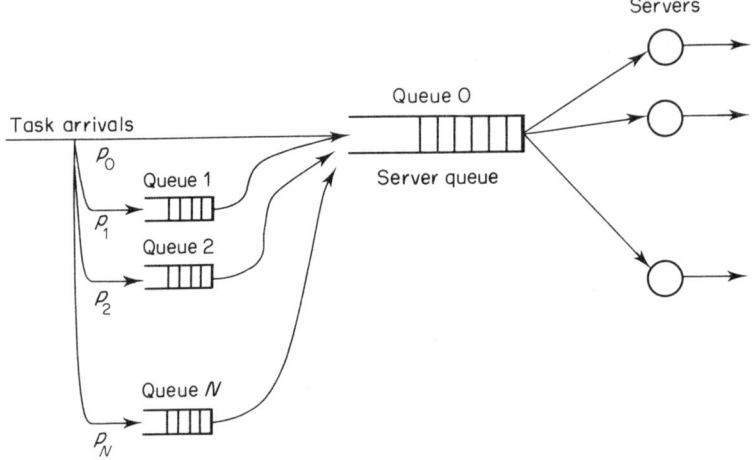

Figure 7.1: The model description

7.3 Derivation of the Job Response Time

The determination of the response time of a job described by a task graph G (i.e. the overall delay of graph G's tasks through the system), denoted by R_G, is of crucial importance in qualifying the performance of parallel processing. However hardly any theory exists to tackle such problems. The problem seems to be open in its general form.

In order to obtain a tractable solution to the model, we restrict our attention to the simplified model for which the following two major assumptions have been made in Section 7.2:

A1 Every buffer is replaced by a First-Come-First-Served queue. The service time of queue i $(1 \leq i \leq N)$ is exponentially distributed with parameter μ_i which is given below in (7.2). When a task of queue i is released (or completes its 'service'), it joins queue 0 (the multiprocessor queue).

A2 The arrivals of tasks to the system constitute a Poisson process of parameter Λ, $\Lambda = m\lambda$. Let $T_1, T_2, \ldots, T_n, \ldots$ be the arriving tasks. We assume that tasks $T_{im+1}, T_{im+2}, \ldots, T_{im+m}$ belong to the same precedence graph ($i = 1, 2, \ldots$). Upon arrival, a task enters queue j ($0 \leq j \leq N$) with probability $p_j = m_j/m$.

With assumptions **A1** and **A2**, we obtain a product form network of queues which provides the basis of our approach.

7.3. Derivation of the Job Response Time

Before proceeding with the analysis, we introduce the following notation:

- $P(k)$: joint stationary queue length probability distribution,
- $P_i(k_i)$: stationary probability for queue i ($0 \leq i \leq N$) to have k_i ($k_i = 0, 1, 2, \ldots$) customers,
- $E(k_i)$: mean number of tasks in queue i ($0 \leq i \leq N$),
- $E(k)$: mean number of tasks in the system,
- W_i: mean response time of tasks in queue i ($0 \leq i \leq N$),
- W: mean response time of tasks in the system,
- Q: mean number of jobs in the system,
- R: mean response time of a job or program which is represented by the graph G,
- $\bar{w}_j$: expected waiting time of j tasks which arrive simultaneously to queue 0,
- q_i: 'service contribution' to queue i ($0 \leq i \leq N$) of a customer leaving queue 0.

Let V be the set of nodes of graph G, $Suc(v)$ the set of successors and $rank(v)$ the number of predecessors of node v. q_i is defined as the average number of successors having i predecessors:

$$q_i = \frac{1}{m}\left(\sum_{v \in V} \sum_{v' \in Suc(v)} \mathbf{1}(rank(v') = i)\right)$$

where $\mathbf{1}(x)$ is the characteristic function:

$$\mathbf{1}(x) = \begin{cases} 1, & \text{if } x \text{ is true} \\ 0, & \text{if } x \text{ is false} \end{cases}$$

We shall represent the effect of the departure of a task from the system on the set of waiting tasks, as the departure of (q_i/i) tasks on the average from the set of tasks in the ith waiting queue in order to join queue 0. This leads to the expression:

$$\mu_i = \gamma q_i / i \tag{7.2}$$

where γ is the computed effective departure rate from the multiprocessor service queue:

$$\gamma = \sum_{j=1}^{\infty} \mu_0(j).P_0(j) \qquad (7.3)$$

Our approximate model will be an open product-form network; therefore we will use the following formula for the joint queue length probability distribution using the well known product form theorem [1]:

$$P(\mathbf{k}) = C \prod_{i=0}^{N} \prod_{n=1}^{k_i} \frac{\Lambda.e_i}{\mu_i(n)}$$

where C is a normalizing constant, μ_0 is given by (7.1) and the remaining parameters are the average number of visits to each queue:

$$e_0 = 1$$

$$e_i = p_i, \quad \text{if } 1 \leq i \leq N$$

and for $1 \leq i \leq N$:

$$\mu_i(n) = \mu_i, \quad n = 1, 2, \ldots$$

We may write $P(\mathbf{k})$ as follows:

$$P(\mathbf{k}) = \prod_{i=0}^{N} P_i(k_i)$$

where the

$$P_i(k_i) = C_i \prod_{n=1}^{k_i} \frac{\Lambda.e_i}{\mu_i}, \quad i = 0, \ldots, N$$

are the marginal probability distributions and the C_i are their normalizing constants:

$$C_i = \left(\sum_{k_i \geq 0} \prod_{n=1}^{k_i} \frac{\Lambda e_i}{\mu_i(n)} \right)^{-1}$$

These formulae lead to the following computational procedure which will be used to obtain the model's queue length probability distributions:

(1) $P_0(j)$ is obtained formally using

$$P_0(j) = C_0 \prod_{n=1}^{j} \frac{\Lambda}{\mu_0(n)}$$

7.3. Derivation of the Job Response Time

(2) For each $i = 1, 2, \ldots, N$ we compute

$$\mu_i = \frac{q_i}{i} \sum_{j=1}^{\infty} \mu_0(j) \cdot P_0(j)$$

(3) We can now calculate

$$P_i(k_i) = C_i \prod_{n=1}^{k_i} \frac{\Lambda p_i}{\mu_i}, \qquad i = 1, \ldots, N$$

using steps (1) and (2).

For $(i = 0, \ldots, N)$, the mean queue lengths are expressed as

$$E(k_i) = \sum_{n=1}^{\infty} n \, P_i(n)$$

Therefore the average mean number of tasks in the system $E(k)$ is given by

$$E(k) = \sum_{i=0}^{N} E(k_i)$$

By Little's well-known formula, we obtain the average response times of tasks in each queue

$$W_i = \frac{E(k_i)}{e_i \Lambda}$$

and the average total response time of a task

$$W = \frac{E(k)}{\Lambda}$$

The above formulae provide performance measures at the task level. In particular, W_i $(i = 1, \ldots, N)$ indicates the time that a task having i predecessors must expect to wait before becoming available for execution (i.e. joining queue 0).

In order to obtain R, the average response time of a program, we introduce the concept of *level* of a node, or task.

The *level* of a node v of a directed acyclic graph, denoted by $L(v)$, is defined as:

- $L(v) = 1$, if v has no predecessors,
- $L(v) = \left(\max_{p \in Pre(v)} L(p)\right) + 1$, where $Pre(v)$ denotes the set of immediate predecessors of node v.

The *level* of a task is considered to be the *level* of the corresponding node in the task graph. The *depth* of a graph, denoted by d, is given by

$$d = \max_{v \in V} L(v)$$

When a task completes its service at the multiprocessor queue (queue 0), on the average q_i tasks which belong to the same program leave queue i to join queue 0; these tasks are all of the immediate predecessors of the departing task. It is not unreasonable to suppose that tasks of a given program which have the same level in the task graph will be serviced at the multiprocessor queue roughly at the same time. Indeed, if all task execution times were identical it would follow that tasks of level i would only be processed after all tasks of level $(i-1)$ had already been served by the multiprocessor. This leads to the following additional simplifying assumption which we shall make.

A3 Tasks of the same level become simultaneously available for execution.

Let $t_1, t_2, \ldots, t_u$ be a group of tasks simultaneously arriving to the multiprocessor service queue. Without loss of generality, we assume that their service order is $t_1 \prec t_2 \prec \ldots \prec t_u$ where $a \prec b$ means that task b *cannot* execute before a. Let $w_k(n)$ denote the mean waiting time of task t_k $(1 \leq k \leq u)$ before service if there are n $(n = 0, 1, 2, \ldots)$ tasks in the queue at the instant of the arrival of the group. Thus we have the formula

$$w_k(n) = \begin{cases} 0, & \text{if } n \leq M - k \\ (n + k - M)\mu^{-1}/M, & \text{if } n \geq M - k + 1 \end{cases}$$

Therefore, for $j = 1, 2, \ldots$, the expected waiting time of j concurrent tasks in the server queue can be expressed as

$$\bar{w}_j = \sum_{n=0}^{\infty} P_0(n) \, w_j(n)$$

or
$$\bar{w}_j = \sum_{n=\max(M-j+1,0)}^{\infty} P_0(n)\,(n+j-M)\,\mu^{-1}/M \qquad (7.4)$$

Let $b(l)$ denote the number of tasks of level l ($1 \leq l \leq L_G$). According to assumption **A3**, tasks are serviced level by level, and tasks of the same level arrive at the same time to the multiprocessor queue. Therefore the response time R of the parallel program may be expressed as the sum of the completion times of the tasks at each level:

$$R = \sum_{l=1}^{d} \left(\frac{1}{\mu} + \bar{w}_{b(l)}\right)$$

And finally, by Little's formula, the average number of jobs in the system Q, is expressed as
$$Q = \lambda\,R$$

7.4 Numerical Examples and Model Validation

In this section we shall compare the predictions of the model described in this chapter with simulation results. The latter are based on a realistic simulator where parallel programs arrive to a multiprocessor queue with M exponential servers, each of service rate μ. The program arrival process is Poisson of rate λ and the parallel programs are described by a task graph. Simulation runs have been carried out so as to obtain the 95% confidence intervals in each case.

As a first example, consider the parallel program represented by Graph 3 shown in Figure 7.3, together with the other graphs used in the simulations. Its average response time as a function of system load $m\lambda/\mu M$ is plotted in Fig. 7.2 using the prediction of our mathematical model, and the results obtained from simulation experiments, for different values of the number of processors M.

Clearly the theoretical predictions are optimistic with respect to the more realistic simulation results. However, the discrepancy between the two does not appear to be excessive.

In Tables 7.1 to 7.5 we have presented similar results for five different program graphs (Graph 1 to Graph 5). The relative differences in average response time of the program between the mathematical model and the simulation can be less than 2% and as large as 30%. By and large, the difference appears to be less than 20%.

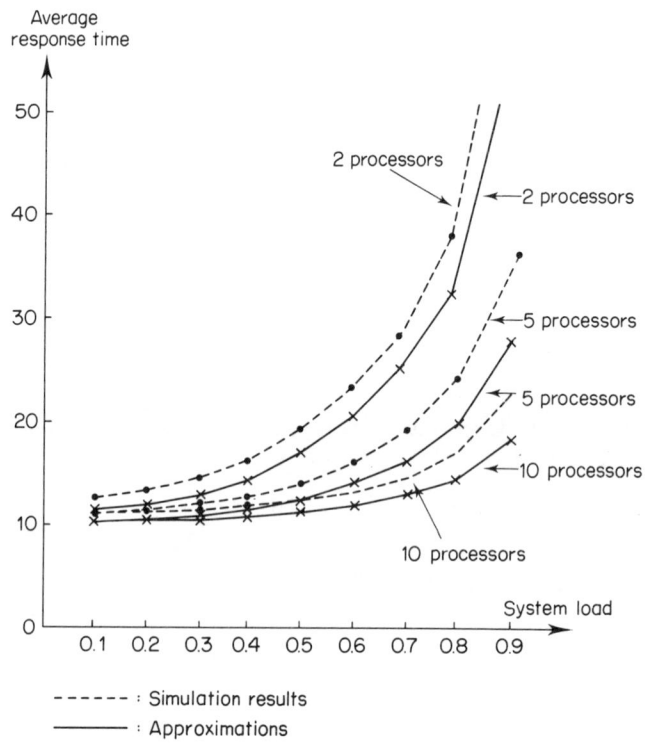

Figure 7.2: Response times of Graph 3 under different system load conditions

Number of processors	System load	Approximate solution	Simulation estimate	Relative error %
1	0.720	32.57	46.84 ± 2.45	30.3
2	0.360	11.19	12.21 ± 0.22	8.3
3	0.485	8.71	9.27 ± 0.09	6.1
5	0.240	8.02	8.39 ± 0.06	4.4
10	0.072	8.00	8.30 ± 0.06	3.6

Table 7.1: Comparison of job response time for Graph 1 ($\lambda = 0.06$, $\mu = 1$)

7.4. Numerical Examples and Model Validation

Number of processors	System load	Approximate solution	Simulation estimate	Relative error %
1	0.960	184.00	241.30 ± 36.23	23.7
2	0.480	14.13	17.69 ± 0.44	20.2
3	0.320	10.85	12.48 ± 0.18	3.1
5	0.192	7.35	10.49 ± 0.07	30.0
10	0.096	7.00	10.21 ± 0.06	31.4

Table 7.2: Comparison of job response time for Graph 2 ($\lambda = 0.06$, $\mu = 1$)

Number of processors	System load	Approximate solution	Simulation estimate	Relative error %
1	0.960	256.00	260.20 ± 37.61	1.6
2	0.480	14.94	18.69 ± 0.44	20.1
3	0.320	10.92	13.78 ± 0.16	20.8
5	0.192	10.03	12.59 ± 0.08	20.3
10	0.096	10.00	12.49 ± 0.07	19.9

Table 7.3: Comparison of job response time for Graph 3 ($\lambda = 0.06$, $\mu = 1$)

Number of processors	System load	Approximate solution	Simulation estimate	Relative error %
1	0.900	78.00	134.30 ± 14.89	41.9
2	0.450	12.78	16.10 ± 0.45	20.6
3	0.300	9.79	10.10 ± 0.12	3.0
5	0.180	7.21	8.21 ± 0.06	12.2
10	0.009	7.00	7.89 ± 0.05	11.3

Table 7.4: Comparison of job response time for Graph 4 ($\lambda = 0.06$, $\mu = 1$)

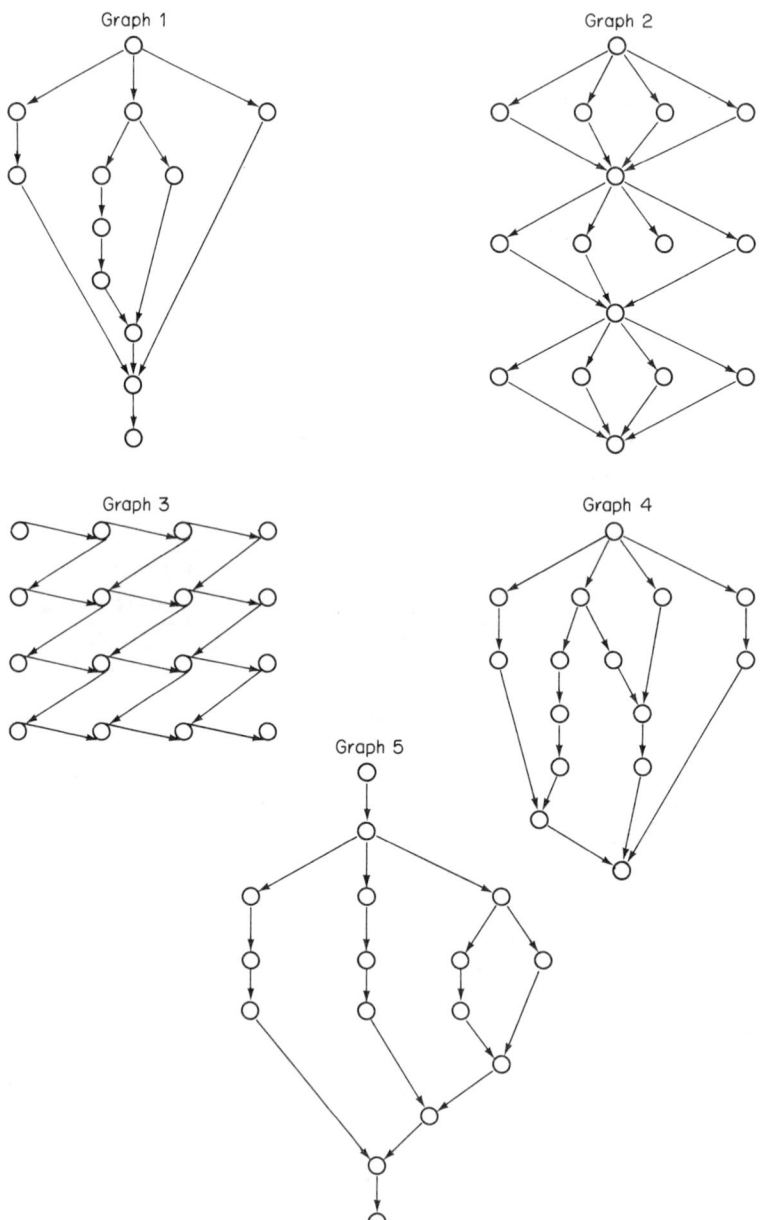

Figure 7.3: Task Graphs 1 to 5 used in the simulation experiments

7.5. Extension of the Method to the Analysis ...

Number of processors	System load	Approximate solution	Simulation estimate	Relative error %
1	0.960	208.00	296.10 ± 44.88	29.8
2	0.480	14.75	18.32 ± 0.52	19.5
3	0.320	11.06	11.79 ± 0.19	6.2
5	0.192	8.25	9.36 ± 0.06	11.9
10	0.096	8.00	8.98 ± 0.05	11.0

Table 7.5: Comparison of job response time for Graph 5 ($\lambda = 0.06$, $\mu = 1$)

The fact that the approximation seems to underestimate the overall average response time can be explained by the three simplifying assumptions. Indeed:

- Bulk arrival queueing systems in general will behave worse than single arrival systems under the same load, with respect to the response time.
- Dependent services (in our model, services of queue 1 to N) generally imply a larger variance of service time, so that the waiting time is greater.
- Synchronization of tasks introduces additional delays over and above the task execution times.

These intuitive arguments indicate that our approximation method provides reasonably lower estimates to the expected response time of parallel programs.

7.5 Extension of the Method to the Analysis of Multiprocessor Systems with Different Types of Parallel Programs

The model we have discussed so far concerns systems in which programs arrive at random, and are composed of a set of tasks whose precedence graph is fixed and deterministic. Furthermore all programs have the same precedence graph, and all tasks have independent exponentially distributed service times with the same parameter μ.

In many practical cases of interest, different types of parallel programs will run on the same system. In this section we shall consider an extension of our model in order to handle this more general case.

We shall assume now that there are H different types of programs, each type h having a different precedence graph denoted G_h. However, all the tasks will be assumed to have the same exponential processing time distribution of parameter μ. Programs of type h arrive to the system according to a Poisson process of parameter λ_h, and the H different arrival processes are independent.

Programs of class h have m_h tasks which are subdivided into N_h ($N_h \leq m_h - 1$) groups according to their respective number of predecessors' tasks.

We now consider a stream of tasks $t_1, t_2, \ldots, t_n, \ldots$ arriving to the system, where the task t_n belongs to a program of class j with probability $m_j/\sum_1^H m_h$. The global arrival process is Poisson of parameter Λ,

$$\Lambda = \sum_{h=1}^{H} m_h . \lambda_h$$

Upon arrival, a task joins the queue i ($0 \leq i \leq N$) with probability p_i given by

$$p_i = \frac{\sum_{h=1}^{H} m_{hi}}{\sum_{h=1}^{H} m_h}$$

where m_{hi} is the number of tasks in G_h having i predecessors, and

$$\sum_{i=0}^{H} m_{hi} = m_h, \qquad h = 1, 2, \ldots, H$$

The *service contribution* of tasks of rank i for this model becomes

$$q_i = \frac{1}{\sum_{h=1}^{H} m_h \left(\sum_{h=1}^{H} \sum_{v \in G_h} \sum_{v' \in Suc_h(v)} \mathbf{1}(rank(v') = i) \right)}$$

where $Suc_h(v)$ denotes the set of successors of node v in the graph G_h.

We can now use again the previous results for computing the queue length probabilities, mean queue lengths, mean number of tasks in the system, and average delays. Furthermore, the mean number of tasks in the system which belong to jobs of class j ($j = 1, 2, \ldots, H$) in queue i ($i = 1, 2, \ldots, N$), denoted by $E(k_{ji})$, can be expressed as

$$E(k_{ji}) = \frac{m_{ji}\lambda_j}{\sum_{h=1}^{H} m_{hi}\lambda_h} E(k_i)$$

where $E(k_i)$ is obtained as in Section 7.3 with the new values of Λ and q_i. And the mean number of tasks which belong to jobs of class j ($j = 1, 2, \ldots, H$) in the system, denoted by $E(k^j)$, can be expressed as

$$E(k^j) = \frac{m_j \lambda_j}{\sum_{h=1}^{H} m_h \lambda_h E(k)}$$

The average response time of a job of class h is also obtained using the approach developed in Section 7.3. With assumption **A3**, we can write

$$R_h = \sum_{l=1}^{L_k} \left(\frac{1}{\mu} + \bar{w}_{b_h}(l) \right)$$

where R_h denotes the expected response time of a program of class h, L_h denotes the level of graph G_h, $b_h(l)$ denotes the number of tasks in graph G_h at level l ($1 \leq l \leq L_{G_h}$), and $\bar{w}_j$ ($j = 1, 2, \ldots$) is given by (7.4).

The average number of programs of class h in the system is expressed as:

$$Q_h = \lambda_h R_h$$

and the average number of programs in the system is

$$Q = \sum_{h=1}^{H} Q_h$$

We thus obtain a computationally tractable estimate of the average response time of concurrent programs of different types which run on the same multiprocessor system.

7.6 The Case of Systems with Processors of Different Types

Many multiprocessor systems contain processors of different types. Consider for instance the following two examples. Supercomputers will often include three types of processors: scalar arithmetic processors, vector or array (arithmetic) processors, and processors for simple instructions such as jumps, address decoding, etc. Other multiprocessor systems may include specialized processors which handle operating system calls, input-output processors, as well as processors which execute user program code. The connection machine, which is discussed in Chapter 9, includes two types of processors: elementary logical processors and floating-point arithmetic processors.

We thus see that as a general rule multiprocessor systems will contain more than one type of processor. Programs will contain tasks which are directed to different types of processors, for instance floating point instructions and control instructions in a numerical analysis program, if we consider individual instructions to be tasks. Thus we shall consider a class of models with different types of tasks being executed on the corresponding types of processors.

In this section we shall address the analysis of this class of models with dependencies between tasks of the same program.

The general model described in Section 7.2 can also be applied to the case which is of interest to us here. However due to its intrinsic complexity we shall present a simplified model which yields very satisfactory approximate results.

Consider the model shown in Figure 7.4 . It represents a system having K types of processors; there are M_k processors of type k, $(1 \leq k \leq K)$. The arrival of a program to the system is represented by the arrival of a sequence of tasks. Tasks will be represented by customers moving through the queues and their execution times will be represented by service times at the servers. The state of the system will be represented by the vector

$$\mathbf{S} = (n_1, \ldots, n_K, b_1, \ldots, b_K)$$

where $n_1, \ldots, n_K$ are the numbers of tasks in the processor queues $(1, \ldots, K)$, respectively, and $(b_1, \ldots, b_K)$ are the numbers of tasks in the waiting queues $(1, \ldots, K)$, respectively.

The waiting queues contain those tasks, all of whose predecessors have not yet completed execution. A task from waiting queue i will request service from a processor of type i as soon as its predecessors (which may belong to any type) have completed execution. Processors serve the tasks in the processor queues in first-come-first-served order.

We shall assume that all processor service or execution times are independent and exponentially distributed, and that the waiting times in the waiting queue are also independent and exponentially distributed.

Furthermore, arrivals of tasks to the system will be represented by a Poisson process of parameter $\Lambda = \lambda m$, where λ is the rate of arrival of programs to the system (in programs per unit time) and m is the average number of tasks in a program.

7.6. The Case of Systems with Processors ...

We shall denote by m_k the average number of tasks of type k in a program, so that

$$m = \sum_1^K m_k$$

The tasks of a program may or may not have predecessors; thus there will be on the average m_{k_0} tasks of type k without predecessors and m_{k_1} on the average with predecessors, where $m_k = m_{k_0} + m_{k_1}$.

The state transitions of the model from some state S to some state S' are described as follows:

- Arrival of a task.

    The arrival of tasks to the system occur according to a Poisson process with rate $m\lambda$. Upon arrival, a task becomes a customer of processor queue k or of waiting queue k:

    $$S' = (n_1, \ldots, n_k + 1, \ldots, n_K, b_1, \ldots, b_K)$$

    or

    $$S' = (n_1, \ldots, n_K, b_1, \ldots, b_k + 1, \ldots, b_K)$$

    with probability $p_{k_0} = m_{k_0}/m$, and $p_{k_1} = m_{k_1}/m$, respectively. The rates of transition from state S to these particular S's are thus $\lambda m p_{k_0}$, and $\lambda m p_{k_1}$, respectively.

- Departure of a task from one of the waiting queues.

    Departures from the waiting queues form independent Poisson processes. The state transition from S to some

    $$S' = (n_1, \ldots, n_k + 1, \ldots, n_K, b_1, \ldots, b_k - 1, \ldots, b_K)$$

    for $b_k > 0$, occurs with rate $\lambda m p_{k_1}$.

- Departure of a task from a processor queue.

    This will lead into state

    $$S' = (n_1, \ldots, n_k - 1, \ldots, n_K, b_1, \ldots, b_K)$$

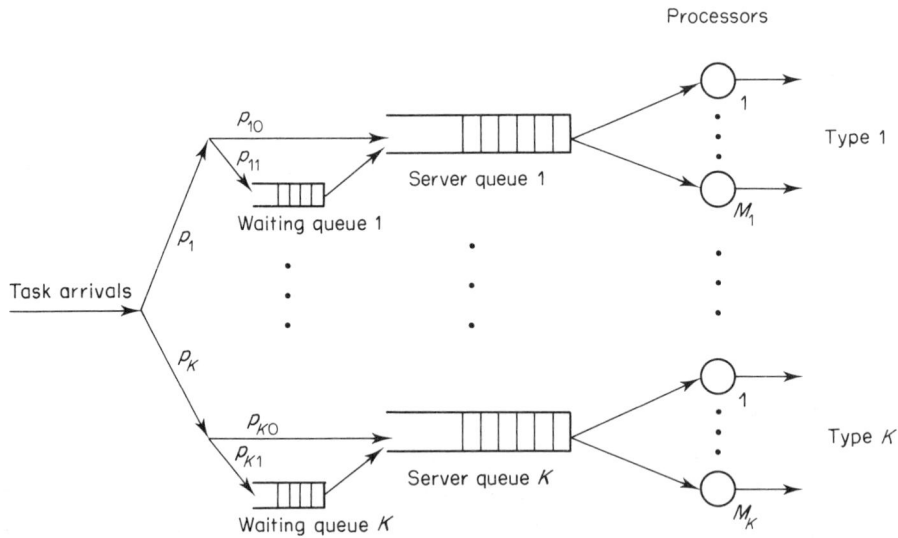

Figure 7.4: Simplified model description for the non-homogeneous processor case

where $n_k > 0$. Such a state transition takes place with rate

$$\mu_k(n_k) = \begin{cases} n_k \mu_k, & \text{if } 1 \leq n_k \leq M_k \\ M_k \mu_k, & \text{if } n_k > M_k \end{cases}$$

No other state transitions, except for those given above, can occur.

The total response time of a program will be derived from the total waiting and execution times of its tasks. These are composed of task precedence waiting times, task queueing times for executions, and task execution times. The precedence waiting times are due to the precedence constraints or the synchronization delays, and are the time needed for tasks to be enabled by their predecessors in the task graph. The queuing times result from waiting for processors.

The program response time will be computed in two steps. We first compute the task response times, and then compute program response time by taking into account the precedence waiting times using the task graph.

From the construction of the simplified model, every server queue forms an $M/M/m$ queueing system, with customer arrival rate $\lambda_k = p_k m \lambda$, where

7.6. The Case of Systems with Processors ...

$p_k = m_k/m$, $(1 \leq k \leq K)$, and with service rate

$$\mu_k(j) = \begin{cases} j\mu_k, & \text{if } 1 \leq j \leq M_k \\ M_k\mu_k, & \text{if } j > M_k \end{cases}$$

The stationary probability distribution of the length of the kth processor queue, $(1 \leq k \leq K)$, denoted by $P_k(n_k)$, is

$$P_k(n_k) = C_k \prod_{j=1}^{n_k} \frac{\lambda_k}{\mu_k(j)}, \qquad n_k \geq 0 \qquad (7.5)$$

where C_k is the normalizing constant:

$$C_k = \left(\sum_{n=0}^{\infty} \prod_{j=1}^{n} \frac{\lambda_k}{\mu_k(j)} \right)^{-1}$$

If there are j tasks (under execution or ready for execution) in the kth processor queue when a task arrives to it, its waiting time is the time which elapses until there are at most $M_k - 1$ tasks before it in queue.

Let $w_t(k, j)$ be the queueing time of task t in queue k if there are $(j \geq 0)$ tasks in the queue when it arrives, and let y_i^k $(i \geq 1)$ be the total time for i departures from queue k, given that all the M_k processors of queue k are busy (i.e., there are always tasks in the queue ready for execution when a processor terminates the execution of a task). Then

$$w_t(k, j) = \begin{cases} 0, & j \leq M_k - 1 \\ y_j^k - M_k + 1, & j \geq M_k \end{cases}$$

If $X_k(x)$ is the probability distribution function of the time between successive departures from queue k given that all M_k processors of queue k are busy, and $Y_i^k(x)$ is the distribution function of y_i^k, then

$$X_k(x) = 1 - e^{-M_k\mu_k x}, \qquad x \geq 0,$$

and

$$Y_i^k = \mathop{\text{\Large *}}_{n=0}^{i} X_k$$

where $*$ denotes convolution in the sense of the densities.

Let $T_k(x)$ $(1 \le k \le K)$ be the probability distribution function of the processing time of tasks on processors of type k, given by

$$T_k(x) = 1 - e^{-\mu_k x}, \quad x \ge 0,$$

and $R_k(x)$ be the probability distribution function of response time of the tasks run on processors of type k. The task response time distribution can be obtained from

$$R_k = \sum_{j=0}^{M_k-1} P_k(j).T_k + \sum_{j=M_k}^{\infty} P_k(j).(Y_{j-M_k+1}^k * T_k) \quad (7.6)$$

In practical terms, the above formula can be approximated by

$$R_k = \sum_{j=0}^{M_k-1} P_k(j).T_k + \sum_{j=M_k}^{Z} P_k(j).(Y_{j-M_k+1}^k * T_k) \quad (7.7)$$

where Z is chosen to be sufficiently large so that

$$\sum_{j=0}^{Z} P_k(j) \sim 1$$

Once the distribution functions $R_k(x)$ of the executions times of tasks is known using (7.7), we can proceed to compute the response time of a program as follows:

(i) We assign to each leaf (a node with no successors) of the task graph, a weight which is the function $R_k(x)$ if the leaf is a task of type k.

(ii) For every node i, all of whose successors already have an assigned weight, we assign a weight $W_i(x)$:

$$W_i(x) = R_k(x) * \prod_{j \in Suc(i)} W_j(x) \quad (7.8)$$

if node i is of Type k. In other words, we calculate the maximum of the weights of its set of successors $Suc(i)$, and then add to it its own execution time. Of course, this is done in terms of the distributions of the times.

7.6. The Case of Systems with Processors ...

This procedure will necessarily stop at the roots of the program graph, since it is acyclic.

The response time of the program will now have the following approximate distribution:

$$W(x) = \prod_{l \in \text{Root}(G)} W_l(x) \qquad (7.9)$$

where $\text{Root}(G)$ is the set of roots of the program graph G. The expression (7.9) is based on the assumption that the paths starting from different roots are quasi-independent so that it is justified to calculate the maximum path length distribution as the product of the individual path length distributions.

This approach is illustrated in the following section.

7.6.1 Application of the Method to a System with Series-Parallel Task Graphs

Series-parallel task graphs as models of parallel program structure have been discussed in Chapter 5. In this section we shall use the method developed above for the evaluation of the response time in a multiple processor system in which the work-load is represented by a set of programs each of which have the same series-parallel task graph structure.

The characteristics of the multiprocessor are as follows:

- It has a total of seven processors.
- They are subdivided into three types ($K = 3$).
- There are three processors of Type 1, two processors of Type 2, and two processors of Type 3 ($M_1 = 3$, $M_2 = 2$, $M_3 = 3$).

The system considered is shown on Fig. 7.5.

The programs arriving to the system have an identical series-parallel structure composed of ten tasks $T_1, \ldots, T_{10}$ as shown on Fig. 7.6, with the following characteristics:

- Tasks $T_1, T_3, T_5, T_9, T_{10}$ are of Type 1.
- Tasks T_2, T_4, T_8 are of Type 2.
- Tasks T_6, T_7 are of Type 3.

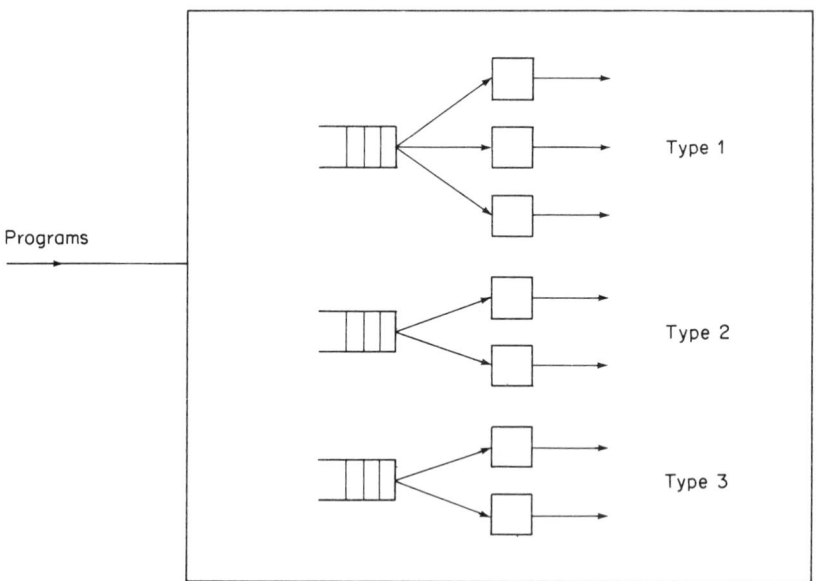

Figure 7.5: Multiprocessor system example

- Type 1 tasks have an average processing time of 1 $\mu_1 = 1$
- Type 2 tasks have an average processing time of 2 $\mu_2 = 0.5$
- Type 3 tasks' average processing time is 3 $\mu_3 = 0.33$.

If the arrival rate of programs to the multiprocessor system is λ, then we will have
$$\lambda_1 = 5\lambda, \quad \lambda_2 = 3\lambda, \quad \lambda_3 = 2\lambda,$$
and we use (7.5) to obtain the stationary queue length distribution at each of the three processor queues.

The average response time is now calculated using the method of this section as a function of system load ρ defined as
$$\rho = \max_k \frac{\lambda m_k}{M_k \mu_k}$$
Notice that ρ describes the maximum load for any type of processor. It can be readily seen that
$$\frac{m_1}{M_1 \mu_1} = 1.67, \qquad \frac{m_2}{M_2 \mu_2} = 3, \qquad \frac{m_3}{M_3 \mu_3} = 3$$

7.7. Bibliography

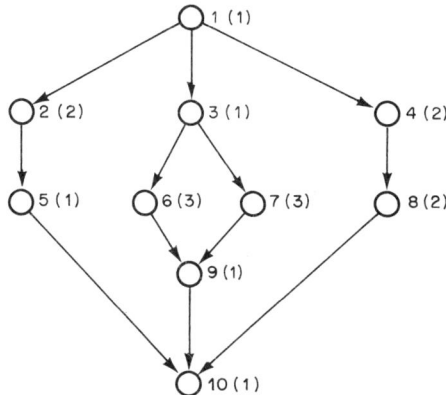

Figure 7.6: The example series-parallel program structure with ten tasks

so that ρ will be determined by processors and tasks of Type 2 and 3. The results concerning the response times are shown on Figure 7.7 where the analytical approximation method is compared with simulation results; the latter are estimated with 95% confidence. The analytical approximation is seen to be highly accurate.

7.7 Bibliography

There has been much interest in the performance evaluation of multiprocessor systems with concurrent programs in recent years. A concurrent program consists of a set of interdependent tasks with precedence constraints which are usually described by a task graph, also referred to as a precedence graph, whose nodes represent tasks and whose directed edges represent precedence relations between tasks. One of the most important performance measures considered is the overall response time of a concurrent program running on multiprocessor systems.

When the duration of tasks is fixed and there are infinitely many processors, it is easy to determine the completion time of a concurrent program by using PERT diagrams. If resources are limited, results, discussed in Chapter 8, exist in the area of task assignment and task scheduling. When task durations are allowed to be random, the performance analysis of concurrent programs becomes more difficult.

In order to make the analysis tractable, simple structures have been considered. Robinson[2], and Sahner and Trivedi [6] obtain the overall execution time by restricting the graph structure to be *series-parallel*. Gelenbe et al.

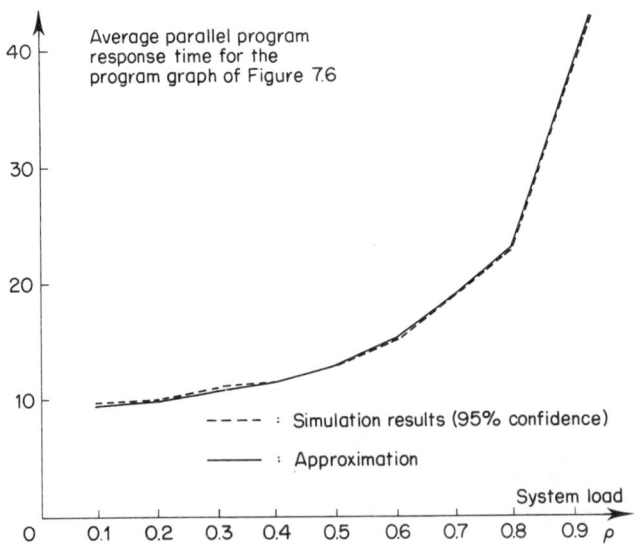

Figure 7.7: Mean job response times under different system load conditions

[4] consider the same graph structure with random graph models and derive a closed form expression for the maximum speed-up which can be expected by executing such programs on a multiprocessor system.

Dodin [5] studies the general directed acyclic graph structure. By removing edges or splitting nodes, a directed acyclic graph can be transformed into a *series-parallel* graph. Thus lower bounds and upper bounds for overall completion time are obtained.

Studies along similar lines to those presented in this chapter, which are based on the use of queueing network models [1], can be found in [7, 8, 11] where further references are given. The presentation of this chapter is based on the work of Gelenbe and Liu [9, 10].

[1] Baskett, F., Chandy, K.M., Muntz, R.R. and Palacios, F. G. 'Open, Closed and Mixed Networks of Queues with Different Classes of Customers', *J.ACM*, Vol. 22, pp. 248–260 (1975).

[2] Robinson, J. T. 'Some Analysis Techniques for Asynchronous Multiprocessor Algorithms', *IEEE Trans. on Software Engineering*, Vol.SE-5, No.1, pp. 24–31 (January 1979).

[3] Gelenbe, E., Montagne, E., Suros, R. and Woodside, C. M. 'A Perfor-

7.7. Bibliography

mance Model of Block-Structured Parallel Programs', in *Parallel Algorithms and Architectures*, M. Cosnard et al. (eds), North-Holland, Amsterdam, pp. 127–138 (1986).

[4] Gelenbe, E., Nelson, R., Philips, T. and Tantawi, A. 'The Asymptotic Processing Time for a Model of Parallel Computation', *Proceedings of National Computer Conference*, Las Vegas, USA (1986).

[5] Dodin, B. 'Bounding the Project Completion Time Distribution in PERT Networks', *Operations Research*, Vol.33, No.4, pp. 862–881 (July–August 1985).

[6] Sahner, R. A. and Trivedi, K. S. 'Performance and Reliability Analysis Using Directed Acyclic Graphs', *IEEE Trans. on Software Engineering*, Vol.SE-13, No.10, pp. 1105–1114 (October 1987).

[7] Towsly, D., Rommel, C. G. and Stankovic, J. A. 'The Performance of Processor Sharing for Scheduling Fork-Join Jobs on Multiprocessors', in *High Performance Computer Systems*, E. Gelenbe (ed.), North-Holland, pp. 145–156 (1988).

[8] Nelson, R. and Tantawi, A. 'Approximating Task Response Times in Fork-Join Queues', in *High Performance Computer Systems*, E. Gelenbe (ed.), North-Holland, pp. 157–167 (1988).

[9] Gelenbe, E. and Liu, Z. 'Performance Analysis Approximations for Parallel Processing in Multiprocessor Systems', North-Holland, *Proceedings of the IFIP Working Conference on Parallel Processing*, Pisa, Italy (April 1988).

[10] Gelenbe, E. and Liu, Z. 'Performance Analysis Approximation for Multiprocessing of Concurrent Programs', to appear.

[11] Chu, W.W. and Leung, K.K. 'Module Replication and Assignment for Real-Time Distributed Processing Systems', *Proceedings of the IEEE*, Vol. 75, No. 5 (May 1987).

8

Supercomputer Performance Evaluation

8.1 Introduction

Although what one usually calls a supercomputer has not traditionally been a multiprocessor, it is impossible to ignore this very important chapter of high performance computing in a monograph, such as this one, devoted to multiprocessor systems. Furthermore, many present day supercomputer systems, such as the IBM 3090 with the vector processor facility, the ETA GF30, etc., as well as advanced research projects (such as the TERAFLOP-1 of IBM) make use of multiprocessing as well as of the more conventional vector processing facilities.

Novel supercomputers, such as the Connection Machine of Thinking Machines Corp., are in fact very large multiprocessors.

In the present chapter we shall concentrate on relatively conventional supercomputer architectures which combine a small number of scalar and vector processors on the execution of a single job.

In order to set the discussion in this chapter in perspective, in Fig. 8.1 we show the peak as well as the minimum expected processing power, expressed in fractions or multiples of GIGA-FLOPS (10^9 Floating–Point Operations per Second) for some well-known supercomputers, with their dates of appearance on the market. These figures are of course approximate and should not be taken to be exact values at a specific date.

Peak processing power of the order of 100 GIGAFLOPS have been suggested for supercomputers combining both vector and parallel processing in

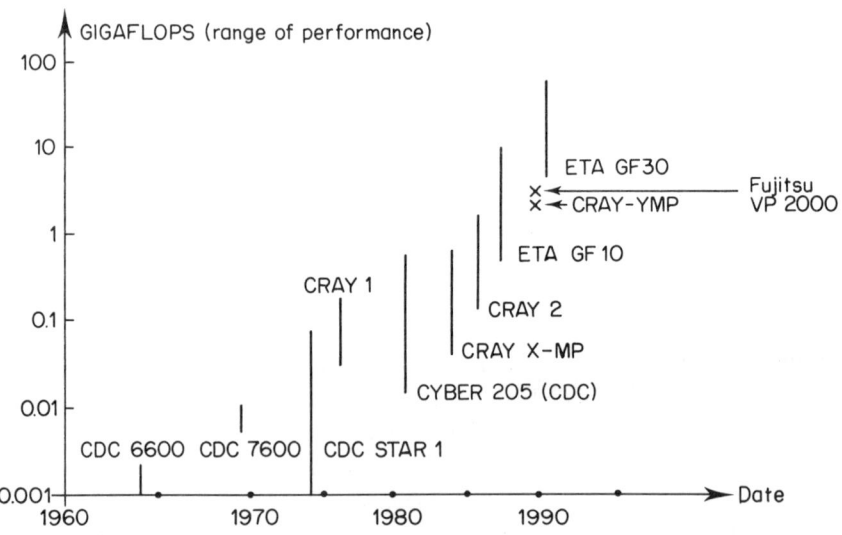

Figure 8.1: Peak and minimum expected power of some well-known supercomputers, with their date of appearance on the market

the foreseeable future.

Such high processing rates are of great use in many important areas of computing. For just one of these application areas, the equations of fluid dynamics which have to be solved when one models the motion of cars or of aircraft, we give below an indication of the total number of Floating−Point Operations which are necessary for their solution as well as a rough indication of solution times (in CPU hours) for the CDC 7600, and for a supercomputer nominally operating at 10 GIGAFLOPS and at 100 GIGAFLOPS.

Problem	CDC 7600	10 GIGAFLOPS	100 GIGAFLOPS
Study of pressure on aircraft body	1 h	0.001 h	10^{-4} h
Aerodynamic noise study	3×10^5 h	30 h	3 h
Energy dissipation in turbulent flows	$3 \times 10^7 - 3 \times 10^{10}$ h	$3 \times 10^4 - 3 \times 10^7$ h	$3 \times 10^3 - 3 \times 10^6$ h

8.2. Performance of a Single Processor

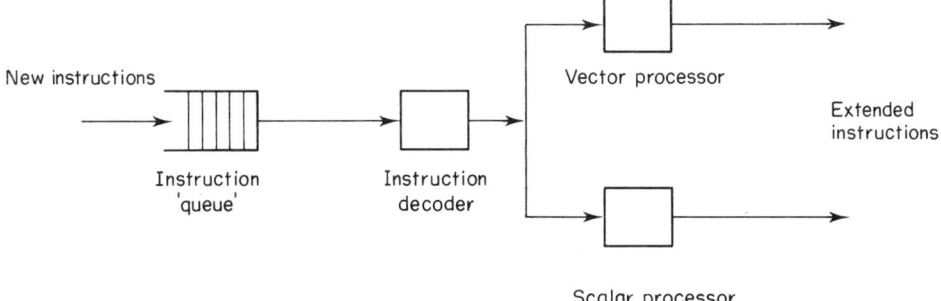

Figure 8.2: A simple array or vector processing architecture

This table shows very clearly that important issues in fluid dynamics are still beyond the reach of state of the art supercomputing even under the assumption that massive parallel processing is used.

In the sequel we shall use performance models in order to understand the intrinsic potential and limitations of supercomputers. We shall orient our discussion towards the execution of programs which contain a large number of array (i.e. vector or matrix) operations, since these are the primary target of supercomputers.

8.2 Performance of a Single Processor

The simplest 'supercomputer' we shall consider is composed of the architecture shown in Fig. 8.2.

Here an imaginary instruction queue stores all the instructions of a program; they are fetched by the instruction decoder which examines them to determine whether the vector processor or the scalar processor is concerned by a particular instruction. Once the choice is made, the instruction is transferred to the appropriate processor for execution. We can now determine in simple terms what the effective processing speed (in number of instructions per second) will be. For the sake of simplicity let us assume that both processors are executing floating-point operations. All execution times considered will include the time needed to fetch instructions and data from main memory, and the time needed to store the results.

Let d be the time necessary to fetch and decode an instruction; v and s will be the time necessary for a vector and scalar operation, respectively. Let us first assume v to be independent of the actual size of the arrays concerned; in fact this is not realistic and the constraint will be removed in Section 8.4. In general, the vector processor will only be able to handle arrays whose size is smaller than some maximum value. The time it will take to fetch, process, and then store the data (after execution), will often vary with the size of the arrays being actually handled; this is a consequence of several factors, including possible memory interference and the manner in which the elements of the array processor are loaded and unloaded. We shall denote by α the actual number of operations executed on the average by the vector processor at each of its execution steps. Finally let p_v and p_s be the proportion of vector and scalar instructions contained in the program; clearly we have $p_s = 1 - p_v$ in the present model. We thus see that an instruction will be executed in an average time given by

$$t_I = d + vp_v + s(1 - p_v)$$

Similarly, the average number of operations executed in one operation will be

$$n_I = \alpha p_v + 1(1 - p_v)$$

The number of operations executed per unit time (or processing power) will then be

$$n = \left(\frac{\alpha}{d+v} - \frac{1}{d+s}\right) p_v + \frac{1}{d+s} \tag{8.1}$$

In many architectures it may be possible to pipe-line the processing of instruction decode with the instruction execution; since it is reasonable to assume that $d < v$ and $d < s$, the instruction decode time d will then not be perceived in the average instruction execution time. In some other cases, there may be the possibility of executing successive instructions in parallel if they are of different type (i.e. vector and scalar); let q be the proportion of successive instructions which are of different type and which can be executed in parallel. This yields the following upper bound to the processing power of the system:

$$n' \leq \left(\frac{\alpha}{v} p_v + \frac{1}{s} p_s\right)(1-q) + \left(\frac{\alpha}{v} + \frac{1}{s}\right) q$$

In Fig. 8.3 we plot n' against the ratio α/v for $d = 0$ and $s = 1$ for various values of p_v and q. As one would expect, we see that the system performance is very sensitive to the ratio α/v or effective number of operations per second for vector operations, and to the proportion p_v of vector operations.

The time v is approximately 11 μs on a CDC CYBER 205 and 30 μs for a CRAY-1 computer for a 1000 element vector. We are thus dealing with values of α/v which will be of the order of 100 MFLOPS (10^8 Floating Point Operations per Second) or 0.1 GIGAFLOPS for a single vector processor.

8.3. *Supercomputers with Multiple Vector Processors* 125

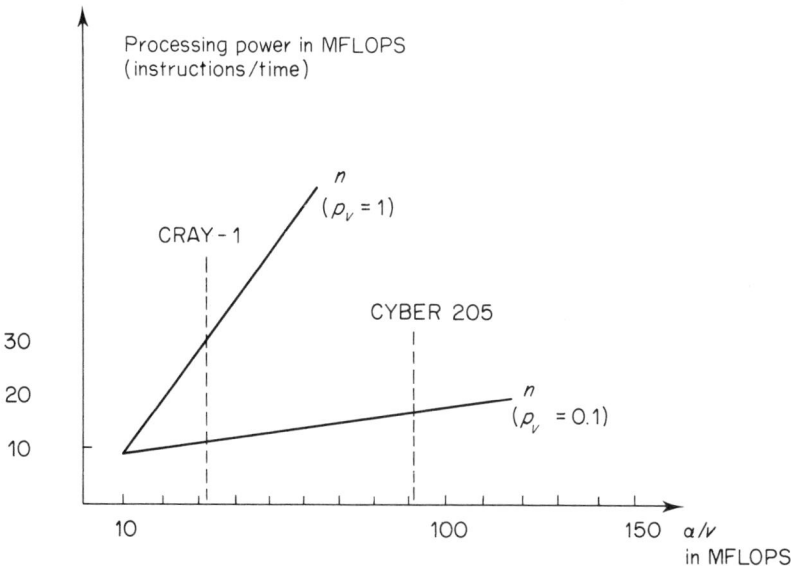

Figure 8.3: Processing power of a simple vector as a function of α/v and of the proportion of vector operations

8.3 Supercomputers with Multiple Vector Processors

In general, large scale supercomputing facilities will include several vector processors and possibly several scalar processors as shown in Fig. 8.4.

In such systems, problems related to access to high-speed memory can become a major limitation to performance. Indeed, when a single vector processor accesses main memory it becomes necessary to transfer in parallel a large number of data units so that the slow-down due to memory conflicts will arise as soon as the size of the vector exceeds the number of independently accessible memory units. This situation becomes worse as the number of vector processors increases. In some supercomputers (such as the CYBER 205) memory is accessed directly by the vector processor, while in others (such as the CRAY-1) data is first transferred to registers associated with each functional element of the vector processor; the latter is known as the R-R (register to register) scheme and it may be combined with pipelining in order to alleviate the adverse effects of simultaneous memory accesses.

In fact one may imagine that two sets of registers could be associated

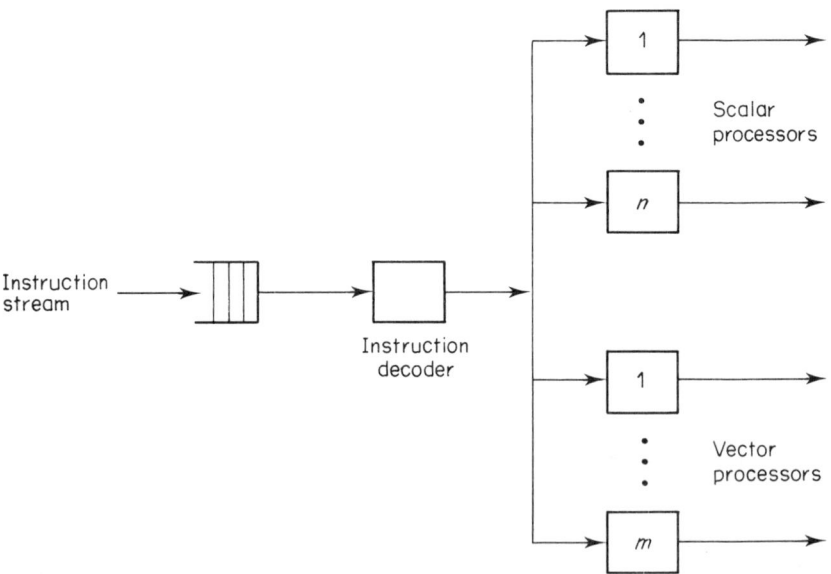

Figure 8.4: Supercomputer with n scalar processors and m vector processors

with a vector processor using a look-ahead scheme to store vector operands in advance in one of the register sets while the other is being used in the course of execution.

Clearly, the capacity to make use of a multiprocessor vector and scalar facility on a single application program will depend to a large extent on the internal structure of the application. This is the issue we shall now address in the rest of this section. In order to do this we shall have to choose an appropriate model of parallel program behaviour, which will be a modification of the task-graph model described in Chapter 6.

The set of instructions of a program will be described by a directed acyclic graph containing K nodes; each node will represent some task. These nodes will be numbered $1, ..., K$ so that node 1 has no predecessor nodes and node K has no successors. Node i may be a predecessor of nodes $i+1, ..., K$, but not of any node j such that $j < i$. Each node or task will be of one or two types : a single scalar instruction (with probability p_s) or a single vector instruction (with probability $p_v = 1 - p_s$). Thus each node in the task graph will represent a single instruction (rather than a set of instructions as in Chapter 6). For $i > j$, an arc from node i to node j will exist with probability p and the existence of any two arcs will be independent.

8.3. Supercomputers with Multiple Vector Processors

If a node represents a vector instruction, then it will operate on the average on α operands; this allows us to assume that some of the vectors being manipulated will not have the full size allowed by the vector processors.

As in the previous sections let v and s be the execution times for vector and scalar instructions, respectively. The average execution time for an instruction will then be

$$t_I = sp_s + vp_v = (v-s)p_v + s$$

where we assume that the time d necessary to decode an instruction is either negligible, or that decoding is being pipelined with executions. Finally, we shall assume that the execution times of tasks are independent random variables with exponential distribution of average value t_I in order to be able to make use of the analytical results of Chapter 6.

Let us first assume that the numbers of scalar and vector processors in the processor being considered is larger than the number actually needed during the execution of a program. Using the results of Chapter 6, we know that the average execution time τ of a program under these assumptions is given by the following approximate formula:

$$\tau \cong \frac{2p}{1+p} K t_I \qquad (8.2)$$

During the complete execution of a program, the total number of instructions executed will be on the average

$$I = K p_s + \alpha K p_v$$

since there will be on average Kp_s scalar instructions and Kp_v vector instructions, or

$$I = K(\alpha - 1)p_v + K \qquad (8.3)$$

Therefore the total processing power in instructions per unit time during this execution will have the following average value:

$$n = \frac{I}{\tau} \cong \frac{(\alpha-1)p_v + 1}{2p((v-s)p_v + s)}(1+p) \qquad (8.4)$$

In order to illustrate this formula, we have chosen figures *close* to those of the CYBER 205 technology : $s = 1$ μs, $v = 11$ μs, and we have plotted n (in GIGAFLOPS) against p_v for various values of α (average vector size) and p (the measure of the degree of parallelism) on Fig. 8.5.

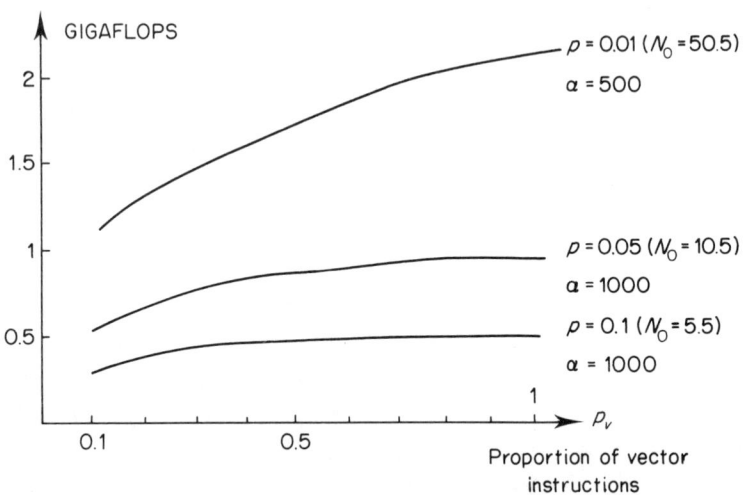

Figure 8.5: Average processing power (in GIGAFLOPS) as a function of the proportion of vector instructions for various values of average vector size α and measure of parallelism p

Notice that the parameter p is related to the degree of parallelism N_0, or average number of tasks which are executed in parallel, defined in Chapter 3 by the relation

$$N_0 \cong \frac{1+p}{2p}$$

or

$$p \cong \frac{1}{2N_0 - 1}$$

so that the total processing power of expression (8.4) may also be written as

$$n \cong N_0 \frac{(\alpha - 1)p_v + 1}{(v - s)p_v + s}$$

8.4 Supercomputers with a Limited Number of Vector Processing Facilities

In the previous section we have considered the performance of a supercomputer in which the number of vector and scalar processors is not a limiting

8.4. Supercomputers with a Limited Number ...

factor. Of course in many real systems the number of processors of either type can be smaller than the number which a parallel program would actually be able to use. This is the case which will be discussed in the present section.

Let us recall the program behaviour model we adopt. A parallel program is composed of K individual instructions; each one is either vector type with probability p_v or of scalar type with probability $p_s = 1 - p_v$. Vector instructions are composed of α operations on the average, and the average execution time of a vector instruction is v, where v can of course depend on α. The average execution time of a scalar instruction is s. The instructions in the parallel program are related by a precedence graph, as introduced in Chapter 6, with probability p for the existence of a precedence of instruction i with respect to j, $(i < j)$.

Assuming that such a program executes with an unlimited number of processors of either type. Its execution will then proceed in virtual time, from some instant 0 to some instant T when execution is complete. In the previous section we have used the expression (see (8.2))

$$\tau = E[T]$$

At any instant t in virtual time, provided that the number of processors is unlimited, there will be $n(t)$ active (i.e. executing) parallel instructions of which $n_v(t)$ will be of vector, and $n_s(t)$ will be of scalar type. On the average during the execution there will be

$$I_v \simeq p_v \frac{1+p}{2p} = p_v N_0 \qquad (8.5)$$

vector instructions executing simultaneously, if the number of vector processors N_v in the system exceeds the number of simultaneously executable (i.e. parallel) vector instructions.

Let us now consider a number of cases of interest where either the scalar or vector processors are less than the number required for a full parallel execution.

8.4.1 N_v vector processors and an unlimited number of scalar processors

In this case let $P_e(N_v)$ be the proportion of time during the execution during which the number of simultaneously executable parallel vector instructions exceeds N_v. Then the average total execution time denoted by τ_1 will be bounded from below as follows:

$$\tau_1 \geq \tau(1 + p_v P_e(N_v)) \tag{8.6}$$

Thus, the processing power n_1 for this class of programs will be bounded from above by the following expressions:

$$n_1 = \frac{I}{\tau_1} \leq \frac{(\alpha-1)p_v + 1}{N_0((v-s)p_v + s)(1 + p_v P_e(N_v))}$$

or

$$n_1 \leq \frac{n}{1 + p_v P_e(N_v)} \tag{8.7}$$

8.4.2 N_v vector processors and a single scalar processor

In many realistic supercomputer architectures, there may be a single scalar processor and a limited number of vector processors. In that case we can easily obtain the following bounds. The average program execution time τ_2 must now satisfy:

$$\tau_2 \geq \tau(p_s N_0 + p_v P_e(N_v))$$

so that the average processing power n_2 is bounded from above:

$$n_2 \leq \frac{n}{N_0 p_v [P_e(N_v) - N_0]} \tag{8.8}$$

8.4.3 The improvement resulting from the use of a larger number of processors

In many cases, when a class of applications is transferred to a system having a larger number of vector processors, the programmer can take advantage of this new situation by splitting certain vector operations into a larger number of simultaneously executing vector operations. This approach will not always improve performance substantially as we now proceed to show. For certain supercomputers which are of 'memory- memory' type, i.e. which execute vector operations directly in memory (like the CYBER 205), the execution time for a vector operation is given by the formula

$$v \cong \mathbf{a} + \mathbf{b}\alpha$$

8.4. Supercomputers with a Limited Number ...

where a and b are constants, and α is the average vector length. Assuming that we have an unlimited number of scalar processors and that $P_e(N_v) = 0$ we have

$$\tau' = [(a + b\alpha)p_v + sp_s]K/N_0 \tag{8.9}$$

for the average execution time of a program.

Now assume that the program is modified so that each vector instruction is split into *two* independent vector instructions. The parameters describing program behaviour will now be modified due to the doubling of vector instructions; the proportion of vector instructions will now be

$$p'_v = \frac{2p_v}{1 + p_v}$$

while N_o will increase as follows:

$$N'_0 = N_0 p_s + 2 N_0 p_v = N_0(1 + p_v)$$

so that the new value of the average execution time becomes after some simplification

$$\tau'' = \frac{K}{N_0}\left[(a + b\frac{\alpha}{2} - s)\frac{2p_v}{1 + p_v} + s\right] \tag{8.10}$$

since $K' = K(1 + p_v)$ is the new value of the total number of instructions. Comparing τ'' with τ' we obtain

$$\frac{\tau''}{\tau} = \frac{(b\alpha + 2a - s)p_v + s}{(1 + p_v)[(b\alpha + a - s)p_v + s]} \tag{8.11}$$

If we can assume that $b\alpha$ is the dominant factor in instruction execution times ($b\alpha \gg a, b\alpha \gg s$), we see that

$$\frac{\tau''}{\tau} = \frac{1}{1 + p_v}$$

so that the gain in processing time is not appreciable if $p_v \approx 0.1$, but can be as high as 50 percent if $p_v \approx 1$.

For instance, when $a + b\alpha$ is $11\mu s$ and $s = 1\mu s$ with $a = 1\mu s$, $p_v = 0.1$, the ratio τ''/τ' is only 0.96.

Therefore the use of a large number of vector processors only seems to provide substantial gain in performance if vector instructions constitute the majority of all operations. In all cases, (8.11) can provide a guideline in making decisions in this respect.

When a register to register scheme is used for vector operations, vector operation execution time is given by the formula

$$v = c + \alpha(e/A + f)$$

where A is the maximum vector size and c, e, f are constants. Again we will be dealing with an expression of the form $v = \mathbf{a} + \mathbf{b}\alpha$ so that the discussion in this section remains valid also for this class of machines.

8.5 Los Alamos Benchmark Characteristics

It is of interest to examine the preceding results in the light of practical data about program behaviour which is derived from the Los Alamos benchmark for supercomputers obtained in [2, 6, 7], as condensed in [9]. We consider the distinct programs from this benchmark and tabulate from [9] their relevant characteristics.

The table shown below lists the characteristics of ten programs in this benchmark.

Program Name	p_v	p_s	$K(\times 10^6)$	α
BMK 1	0.013	0.177	1235.39	61
BMK 4A	0.1905	0.189	143.89	7
BMK 11A	0.011	0.702	292.28	64
BMK 11B	0.021	0.774	199.12	64
BMK 11 C	0.108	0.343	100.42	64
BMK 14	0.052	0.291	52.46	49
BMK 21A	0.0092	0.576	136.04	35
BMK 24A	0.0459	0.349	66.53	31
BMK 24B	0.033	0.362	246.24	63
BMK 24C	0.039	0.357	555.84	47

An important element of information, the degree of parallelism N_0, is not available for these benchmarks. We are dealing here with a vector processor which can only carry out at most 64 operations simultaneously, thus the observed values of average vector size α are quite low. Also we see that

$$p_v + p_s < 1$$

8.5. Los Alamos Benchmark Characteristics

simply because besides the vector and scalar arithmetic operations, the program contains many instructions such as address computations, register transfers, jumps, etc., which are not arithmetic operations; we shall denote by $(1 - p_v - p_s)$ the proportion of instructions of this type.

We now estimate the maximum processing power which may be achieved by programs in the Los Alamos benchmark, but we shall artificially extend the benchmark to include the possibility of parallel processing; this will be represented by the parallelism index N_0. We thus use an instruction execution time of the form

$$t_I = d + vp_v + sp_s + f(1 - p_v - p_s)$$

where d is the time necessary to decode the instruction and f is the execution time of a non-arithmetic instruction. We shall consider a processor architecture where instructions are executed from memory to memory but will consider a technology 10 times faster than the CYBER 205; we then have (in μs)

$$\begin{aligned} v &= 0.1 + 0.01\alpha \\ s &= 0.1 \\ f &= 0.05 \\ d &= 0.01 \end{aligned}$$

so that we are dealing with a processor which executes a floating point operation in 100 nano-seconds. This leads to:

$$t_I = 0.06 + 0.05(p_v + p_s) + 0.01\alpha p_v \quad (\text{in } \mu s).$$

As an example we examine three programs from the Los Alamos benchmark: BMK 1, BMK 4A and BMK 11C. BMK 1 is a very long program, with relatively long vectors but a small proportion of vector instructions. BMK 4A has a large proportion of vector instructions but short vectors, while BMK 11C has a small proportion of vector instructions and long vectors. Call these programs 1, 2 and 3 respectively; their average instruction execution times are given (in μs) as follows:

$$t_{I1} = 0.148, \qquad t_{I2} = 0.092, \qquad t_{I3} = 0.166$$

We now estimate the total number of operations per unit time, or processing power, for each of the three programs. It will be assumed that the number of parallel processors (vector or scalar) which are available exceeds the number which is necessary, and we provide these estimates for two values of the degree of parallelism $N_0 = 2$ and $N_o = 6$.

The processing power in this case will be given by the formula

$$n \cong \frac{I}{Kt_I/N_0}$$

where I, the total number of instructions in a program, is on the average:

$$I = K[1 + (\alpha - 1)p_v]$$

so that

$$n \cong N_0 I/t_I$$

The numerical values are shown below:

Program	Processing power ($\times 10^9$)	
	$N_0 = 2$	$N_0 = 6$
BMK 1	28.030	84.110
BMK 4A	6.708	20.130
BMK 11C	9.440	28.320

This example shows how important the effect of parallelism within the program can be, with a quasi-linear increase in processing power, when a sufficient number of parallel processors is available.

8.6 Bibliography

Some relevant references in the area of supercomputer performance evaluation are given below. The presentation adopted in this chapter does not make direct use of these references, which are based essentially on benchmark studies, except for the data presented in Section 8.5 which was obtained from [9]. In this chapter we have proposed the use of an approach based on artificial workload models. A queueing network approach to supercomputer performance evaluation can be found in [9].

[1] Bucher, I.Y. 'The Computational Speed of Supercomputers', *ACM SIGMETRICS Conference* (1983).

8.6. Bibliography

[2] Bucher, I.Y. and Simmons, M.L. 'Performance Assessment of Supercomputers', in *Vector and Parallel Processors*, M. Ginsberg (ed.), North-Holland (1985).

[3] Dongarra, J., Martin, J. and Worlton, J. 'Computer Benchmarking: Paths and Pitfalls', *IEEE Spectrum* (July 1987).

[4] Griffin, J. and Simmons, M.L. 'Los Alamos National Laboratory Computer Benchmarking 1983', *Technical Report LA-10151-MS* (Los Alamos National Laboratory), New Mexico, USA (1983).

[5] Hwang, K. and Briggs, F.A., *Computer Architecture and Parallel Processing*, McGraw-Hill International Editions (1987).

[6] Lubeck, O., Moore, J. and Mendez, R. 'A Benchmark Comparison of Three Super-computers: Fujitsu VP-200, Hitachi S810/20, and CRAY X-MP/2', *IEEE Computer* (December 1985).

[7] Martin, J., Bucher, I.Y. and Warnock, T.T, 'Workload Characterization for Vector Computers: Tools and Techniques,' *Technical Report LA-UR-83-305* (Los Alamos National Laboratory), New Mexico, USA (1983).

[8] Martin, J. and Mueller-Wichards, D., Supercomputer Performance Evaluation: Status and Directions, *The Journal of Supercomputing*, Vol.1, No.1 (May 1987).

[9] Menasce, D.A. and Almeida, V.A.F. 'On the Investigation of Supercomputer Architectures in Multiprogramming Environments Using Analytic Models', *Technical Report DI-001/88* (Dept. de Informatica, Pontificia Universidade Catolica do Rio de Janeiro), Rio de Janeiro, Brasil (January 1988).

9

Performance Analysis of the Connection Machine

9.1 Introduction

A highly innovative and massively parallel computer system known as the Connection Machine [1] [1, 2] was introduced in the mid-eighties as a new tool for very rapid symbolic processing. Recent experience has shown that this architecture is not only of interest for symbolic or artificial intelligence based applications [14, 15], but that when it is equipped with a sufficiently large number of floating-point processors it is a highly effective tool for large scale numerical computations.

A simplified representation of the Connection Machine (which we designate by CM) is given in Fig. 9.1. The system presented is composed of 64 K (K stands for 1028) or 65 536 processors (P), with 16 K floating–point processors (FP). The system is partitioned into four subsystems of equal size, each of which is controlled separately via a Micro-Controller. The user interface of the system is a set of four host machines.

The CM architecture is perhaps the most novel massively parallel architecture among parallel systems which have been recently developed or proposed [3, 4, 5, 6, 7]. It is a 'logic-in-memory' architecture which does not physically separate the processors from the main memory. Thus, the usual memory to processor communication problem which is of crucial importance to conventional multiprocessor architectures, and which is dealt with by us-

---

[1]The term Connection Machine is a registered trade-mark of Thinking Machines Corporation.

9. Performance Analysis of the Connection Machine

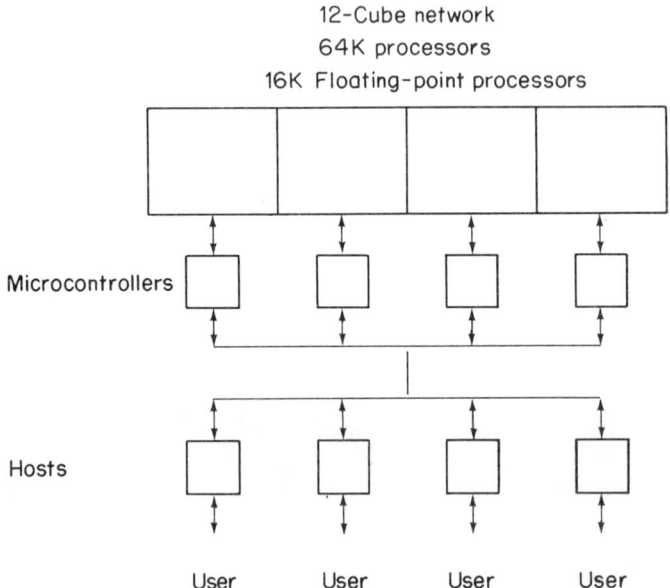

Figure 9.1: General structure of the Connection Machine with four hosts and 64 K processors

ing high performance interconnection networks, does not exist here. On the other hand intense communication needs to take place between the processors, so that the CM is equipped with a sophisticated interprocessor network architecture.

In [1-9] various highly parallel architectures, including the Connection Machine [1,2,8] are described. Communication problems related to such architectures are discussed in [10], while [11-15] present various applications which have been run on the Connection Machine. In [16] the effect of communication on the performance of the Connection Machine is discussed and a queueing network model approach is suggested.

A simplified CM processor interconnection structure is shown in Fig. 9.2.

The key to understanding the architecture of the CM is the communication mechanism used to interconnect the processors. Processors are interconnected in groups of four (P1,P2,P3,P4, or P13,P14,P15,P16, etc.) in a nearest-neighbour network called the NEWS (North–East–West–South) Network. A more complex network called the ROUTER Network is then used to provide a communication path between any pair of processors.

In Fig. 9.2 we have shown a system in which a floating-point processor

9.1. Introduction

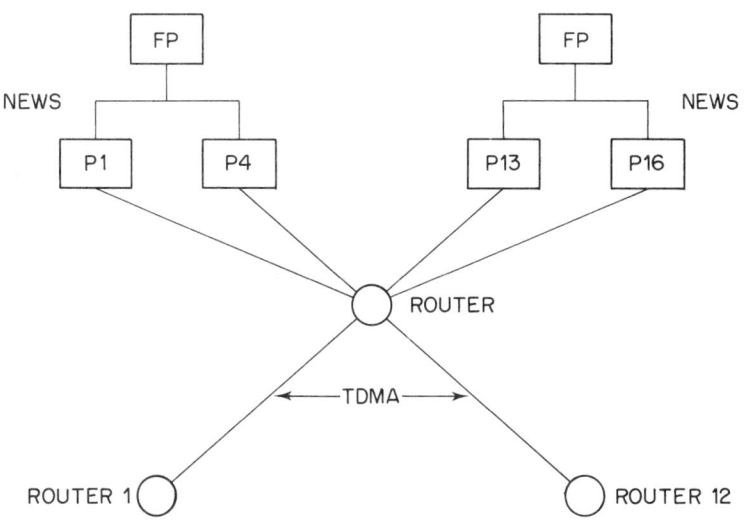

Figure 9.2: Connection Machine processor interconnection structure

(FP) is attached to each NEWS network so that it may be shared among four processors.

Each group of 16 processors, for instance P1 to P16, are connected to the same ROUTER which links them to the rest of the system, and in particular to any other ROUTER, via a 12-Cube network which implements the ROUTER Network.

Each ROUTER is connected to twelve other ROUTERs via bi-directional links. Communication from any ROUTER to these twelve other ROUTERs is carried out in TDMA (Time-Division-Multiple-Access) mode. The TDMA ROUTER Network operates in communication cycles, and during any communication cycle (called a 'petit cycle'), a ROUTER can send a message to *each* of the twelve other ROUTERs to which it is connected, using 12 slots included within one 'petit cycle'.

For a 64 K (65 536) processor machine there will be 4 K (4096) ROUTERs, since 64 K = 16 × 4 K and each ROUTER is connected to 16 processors. Notice that $4096 = 2^{12}$, so that the 12-cube interconnection network allows the connection of all the 4 K ROUTERs [9].

During one single communication cycle, if free time slots are available in the appropriate position of the TDMA algorithm used by the network, a message can travel from any ROUTER to any other ROUTER, passing via intermediate ROUTERs as it progresses through the network. Thus all 4096

ROUTERs are potentially fully interconnected during a single communication cycle.

In reality the communication time may be larger because of traffic in the network. If a given dimension (or direction) slot is occupied at a ROUTER during a given cycle, other messages needing the same direction at a ROUTER will queue up and be transmitted in first-come-first-served order (i.e. the longest waiting message will be transmitted first). A ROUTER may also reject a new message just arriving into the network because its buffer is full. The ROUTER network is guaranteed to deliver messages once they have entered the network using a store-and-forward procedure.

On the other hand, the NEWS network handles local communication between neighbouring processors; it thus reduces the load on the ROUTER network and provides fast local communications between four neighbour processors.

Each elementary processor P is a variable-length operand ALU (arithmetic and logical unit), though this may change in future versions of the machine, and it has a 64 K bit memory. In fact each processor may support up to four resident processes; when this is done throughout the machine, the CM appears as if it is partitioned among four users. Each processor's memory contains a data area and a stack of 1 K bits. Floating-point operations emanating from any one of a set of four processors will be forwarded to the FP for execution without travelling through the ROUTER Network (see Fig. 9.2). Clearly, each of ROUTER 1 to ROUTER 12 of Fig. 9.2 will have the same interconnection structure as the ROUTER placed in the middle of the figure.

Each of the processors executes 'nano-instructions' which are broadcast to all processors via the micro-controllers (see Fig. 9.1). These nano-instructions are generated from macro-instructions which are received by the hosts. Individual processors can be instructed to mask out certain instructions so that it is possible to assign certain computations to certain processors.

Nevertheless, due to the difficulty of addressing a wide variety of instructions to individual processors, the CM architecture is most appropriate for handling SIMD (single-instruction-multiple-data) type parallelism. Thus a stream of instructions is sent from the hosts to a large number of processors simultaneously. Data can be transmitted initially from the hosts to the processors, and intermediate results will then flow between processors via the NEWS and ROUTER networks as the computation progresses.

Clearly, the CM appears to be well adapted to situations in which a small number of distinct instructions have to be executed on a very large data set. Typical examples of this type of computation include operations on very large matrices, image processing, computer vision, etc.

The purpose of this chapter is to examine the effect of communications between processors on the effective processing power of the Connection Machine. The nominal processing power is the number of instructions executed per unit time assuming that all processors are simultaneously busy processing instructions. On the other hand, the effective processing power is the rate of instruction execution when communication slowdowns due to the exchange of messages is included. We assume that the instructions executed, if any, for sending and receiving messages are part of the 'normal' work of a processor, and that therefore these do not contribute to the communications slowdown. However, we obviously consider that the time spent by the processors waiting for messages to arrive from other processors constitutes a source of reductions in the processing power of the machine. Therefore in this chapter we introduce an analytical method to evaluate this reduction. We then present numerical examples to illustrate this effect. Of course, these numerical examples are based on certain parameter choices, such as the nominal instruction execution time of a CM processor, the number of instructions executed between two successive message exchanges, the characteristics of the network, the use of local communications (via the same ROUTER on the network, or within the same NEWS network), etc. Thus these parameters may vary from one application environment to the other. The methodology we propose can be used with other parameter values than those which we introduce in our examples, and our numerical examples are proposed essentially as an illustration of the results.

Since the key element of the CM is the ROUTER Network, in Section 9.2 we present a simple analytical method for evaluating the delay it introduces. The method will be based on an analysis of its performance using existing analytical results in queueing theory. In Section 9.3 we will present a theoretical evaluation of the CM processing capacity using the results of Section 9.2, and a workload model which takes into account the aspects such as the locality of communication patterns among processors.

9.2 ROUTER Network Performance

The structure of the ROUTER Network (RN) has been presented in the previous section. In this section we discuss its performance using a queueing model based on the 'server with vacation times' [17,18].

A message to be sent through the RN will be considered to be a data element which can enter the RN via some ROUTER i and leave it from some ROUTER j in at most 12 communication cycles, or in just one cycle if none of the slots which the message requires as it progresses through the network are already occupied. Notice that because we are dealing with a hypercube, there may be several paths between i and j which are of the same length. We shall denote by k(i,j) the shortest distance, in number of hops, between ROUTER i and ROUTER j and by π the average distance traveled by a message between any two ROUTER's in the ROUTER Network.

Let T be the duration of a communication cycle and by S the length (in time units) of a slot, so that $T = 12S$. A message arriving at a ROUTER and wishing to proceed to some other ROUTER to which it is directly connected (by a single link) observes the following service structure. If the message arrives at an instant when no other message which has arrived before it is directed to the same next ROUTER, it will wait for some time, which will vary between 0 and T, until the appropriate slot comes up; it will then be transmitted during a duration of length S to the appropriate ROUTER. If on the other hand the message finds other messages already waiting for the *same* slot when it arrives, it will be queued until it arrives to the head of the queue and will then be transmitted.

We neglect in our analysis the case where the ROUTER buffer is full so that the message cannot enter its queue. Though this situation is possible in theory, we assume that it is sufficiently unlikely to occur so that it may be neglected. Therefore it will be assumed that all queues considered are of infinite capacity, and blocking at queues is neglected.

The behaviour of the queue of messages at a ROUTER which are directed towards the same neighboring ROUTER (hence using the same slot) is a special case of the queue with autonomous service or of walking type (also known as the queue with server vacations), which is known in the queueing theory literature [17,18]. We shall use a formula derived in [18] to analyse it.

According to these results, and under the only assumption that the arrival of messages to a ROUTER whose destination is a neighbour ROUTER constitute a renewal process (i.e. interarrival times are independent and identically distributed random variables), we can write the following formula for the steady-state *response time* W experienced by the messages (where W denotes the random variable):

9.2. ROUTER Network Performance

$$W = V + T^* + S \tag{9.1}$$

where T^* is a uniformly distributed random variable in the interval $[0, T]$, V is the waiting time which will be detailed below, and V and T^* are independent random variables.

In this formula, V denotes the *waiting time* in a simple queueing system with the same arrival process as the system considered, but with constant service time T; note that the waiting time of a message is defined as the time it waits in queue before receiving service, while its response time is its waiting time plus the transmission time of the message once it has arrived to the head of the queue. As a consequence of (1), the *average response time* of a message is obtained as:

$$E[W] = E[V] + \frac{1}{2}T + S \tag{9.2}$$

Since any given ROUTER receives messages from its twelve neighbouring ROUTERs the arriving message traffic can be expected to be quite random in nature. We shall therefore assume that it is Poisson, since it is the superposition of 12 different and independent arrival processes (it is well known that the Poisson arrival process can be obtained by the superposition of a large number of independent arrival processes). V is then the waiting time of an $M/D/1$ queue (Poisson arrivals and constant service times) and $E[V]$ is obtained from the well-known formula [17]:

$$E[V] = \frac{\lambda T^2}{2(1 - \lambda T)} \tag{9.3}$$

where λ is the number of messages arriving per time unit from the ROUTER Network (RN) which are directed to the particular ROUTER being considered. Finally we have the average response time at the ROUTER:

$$E[W] = \frac{T}{2}\left[1 + \frac{\lambda T}{(1 - \lambda T)}\right] + S \tag{9.4}$$

In order to obtain a measure of the performance of the RN as a whole, we have to know what the average path length Π is for messages entering the network. Clearly we may have a path of length one, if the message leaves the network directly after the first neighbour of the ROUTER from which it entered, or it may be as large as twelve.

For the time being we shall not consider the messages exchanged locally via the ROUTER being considered, between the processors to which it is directly connected. These, and the effect of the NEWS network, will be considered later.

Now assuming that all ROUTER nodes are equivalent with respect to the traffic they carry, we have the RN average response time R to a message which enters it:

$$R = \frac{\Pi T}{2}\left[1 + \frac{\lambda T}{(1-\lambda T)}\right] + \Pi S \tag{9.5}$$

Of course, the *total* traffic coming into ROUTER from the RN will be 12λ on the average if all links carry the same load.

Let us now turn to the traffic *offered* by the processors. Let λ_N be the traffic (always in messages per unit time) which *one* processor sends to the other processors on the same NEWS network. Clearly λ_N will not enter the RN. Let λ_n be the traffic which a processor sends to the twelve other processors which are connected to the same NEWS network (see Fig. 9.2); this traffic may cause congestion at the ROUTER, but it will also not enter the RN and therefore it does not contribute to λ. Finally, we consider the traffic λ_r emanating from a processor and directed to any one of $16 \times (4096 - 1)$ other processors and which can travel from a given ROUTER to a final destination at any one of the remaining 4095 other ROUTERs. Thus a ROUTER will receive on the average, from the processors to which it is directly connected, a traffic of $16\lambda_r$ messages per unit time for transmission over the RN.

Let us examine the relative importance of the quantities involved. In order to optimize the performance of the CM, it is reasonable to assume that a user would attempt to organize his application so that for a given value of $\lambda_N + \lambda_n + \lambda_r$:

- λ_N (the local traffic on the NEWS network) is as large as possible
- then $\lambda_N + \lambda_n$ is as large as possible
- λ_r is as small as possible since it is the traffic which will have the greatest delay
- Π is as small as possible

Furthermore an attempt will be made in the application to share the load equally among ROUTERs, in order to reduce average response times, by using equitable routing through the RN; thus it is reasonable to assume

9.2. ROUTER Network Performance

that the traffic λ carried on all neighbouring links (i.e. 'slot' traffic) is the same. The assumptions may not hold in each particular case but they are valid on the average for a carefully organized application.

We can now relate the link traffic λ to the preceding parameters. Since all traffic emanates from the processors, each ROUTER will receive on the average $16\lambda_r \Pi$ messages per unit time, including messages in transit and fresh incoming traffic from the processors. Assuming that all 12 links are equally loaded we shall have:

$$\lambda = 4\lambda_r \Pi / 3 \tag{9.6}$$

As a consequence and after some simplifications the average response time to messages entering the RN becomes

$$R = \Pi T \left[\frac{7}{12} + \frac{2\lambda_r \Pi T}{(3 - 4\lambda_r \Pi T)} \right]$$

where we have used the fact that $S = T/12$. We see that in order to avoid saturation we must have

$$\lambda_r < \frac{3}{4\Pi T}$$

as the stability (or non-saturation) condition on the average number of messages per time unit that a processor sends into the RN.

The approach we propose here yields, rapidly and in closed form, the average response time or average network traversal time R for the RN. If we choose the time unit to be the duration of the communication (or 'petit') cycle T, i.e. $T = 1$, the formula for R becomes

$$R = \Pi \left[\frac{7}{12} + \frac{2\lambda_r \Pi}{(3 - 4\lambda_r \Pi)} \right] \tag{9.7}$$

This formula will be used in the sequel for the evaluation of the performance of the CM.

If we denote by Λ the total message traffic emanating from a single processor

$$\Lambda = \lambda_N + \lambda_n + \lambda_r$$

then the proportion $f_r = \lambda_r / \Lambda$ of messages sent to other processors via the RN will be an important factor in the performance of the CM. Similarly, the parameter Π will also play an important role.

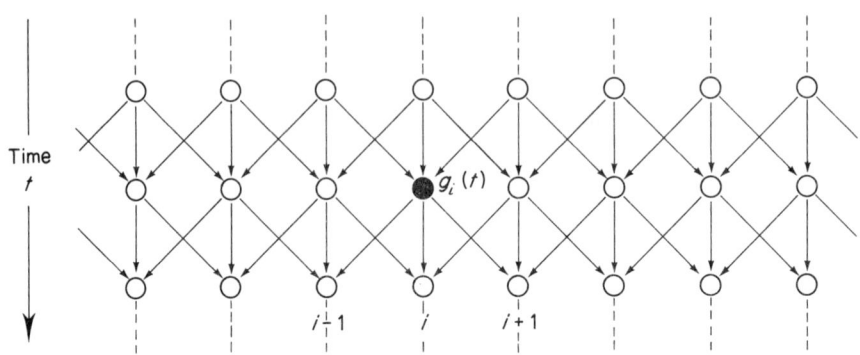

Figure 9.3: A simple highly balanced computation graph

Indeed let ν be the average message delay over the NEWS network, and γ the average message delay for the local interprocessor messages which do not enter the NEWS network or the RN, then the overall average delay D or response time for a message from a processor to its destination will be

$$D = f_N \nu + f_r R + \gamma(1 - f_N) \tag{9.8}$$

where $f_N = \lambda_N/\Lambda$, because *all* messages which *do not* travel through the NEWS network must proceed to the initial ROUTER and then from there to another processor incurring a delay γ; this is not the case for messages which remain on the NEWS network.

The parameters f_N and $f_n = 1 - f_N - f_r$ characterize the computations which only require communications among neighbouring processors; this provides a quantitative characterization of the concept of 'local sphere of computation' introduced in [16].

9.3 Highly Balanced Computations

Intuitively speaking one can expect that the CM performance will be maximized for computations in which each processor carries out the same computational step synchronously with as little communication as possible. The small amount of communication should be carried out among processors which are very close. An example of such a computation, represented by a computation graph, is shown on Fig. 9.3.

In this example, which can represent, for instance, the numerical solution

9.3. Highly Balanced Computations

of the heat equation in one-dimensional space and in time :

$$\frac{\partial g}{\partial t} = a\frac{\partial g}{\partial x} + b\frac{\partial^2 g}{\partial x^2}, \qquad g \equiv g(x,t)$$

each processor handles the computation of $g_i(t)$ for some i, where h is the discretization step of x, and

$$g_i(t) \approx g(ih, t)$$

Thus in the example of Fig. 9.3 processor i computes $g_i(t)$ for discretized time; it receives messages from processors $i-1$ and $i+1$, and sends messages to processors $i-1$ and $i+1$ after each computational step. Other more complex examples of the same general form are frequent in numerical algorithms.

More generally, we shall consider a computational scheme in which that each processor computes for a time C, after which it sends messages for some time m, and then waits for messages for some time M. We shall assume that at each step it sends L messages so that

$$\Lambda = L/(C + m + M)$$

Even for the very simple example of Fig. 9.3 we see that all messages cannot be sent on the NEWS network; indeed each neighbouring group of four processors will send eight messages (we do not consider the information which the processor needs from *itself* and which is represented by the vertical arrow) of which only six can remain on the NEWS network; we thus have $f_N = 0.75$. Similarly we can see that $f_r = 2/32 = 0.0625$.

Assuming perfect synchronization between processors, we shall have M given by the formula for D in (8):

$$M = \gamma + f_N(\nu - \gamma) + f_r \Pi \left[0.583 + \frac{2\Lambda f_r}{(3 - 4\Lambda f_r \Pi)} \right] \qquad (9.9)$$

This equation in fact has the variable M on both sides because Λ is a function of M; it is quadratic in M so that we can solve it easily. Once this is done, we can obtain the processing power η defined as 'Number of Instructions Executed per Unit Time' for the CM on this application as follows. If I instructions are executed in time C by each processor, and if P processors are used by the application (e.g. $P = 16$ K or 64 K), then the processing power η of the CM for this application is given by the formula:

$$\eta = \frac{I.P}{C + m + M} \quad (9.10)$$

where C will of course increase with I, though it will depend on the type of instructions which are being executed in the application. We can use M obtained by substituting (9) in (10) as a function of the parameters of the architecture, namely P, γ and ν, or of those which depend on the architecture of the CM and on the properties of the application such as I, C, m, L, f_r, f_N, Π.

9.3.1 The lightly loaded ROUTER network

For the case when the RN is lightly loaded, i.e. $\Lambda f_r \approx 0$, we have from (9):

$$M = \gamma + f_N(\nu - \gamma) + 0.583\Pi f_r$$

For the sake of simplicity we shall assume that the message delay on the NEWS network is the same as that for messages which go through the ROUTER without passing through the RN: $\gamma = \nu$, so that

$$M = \gamma + 0.583\Pi f_r$$

We then have from (10):

$$\eta = \frac{I.P}{\alpha I + m + \gamma + 0.583\Pi f_r} \quad (9.11)$$

where we have taken $C = \alpha I$ where α is the nominal time needed to execute an instruction. Recall that this formula includes the delay at the RN but assumes that no queues form at the ROUTERs.

In [8] it is indicated that the time necessary to execute a 32 bit add instruction on the CM-2 is 21 μs; therefore we shall choose $\alpha = 21$ if the unit time T is taken to be 1 microsecond.

Let us first assume that $f_r = 0$, so that no messages are being sent in the RN and it has no effect on performance. we then have that the processing power is given by

$$\eta' = \frac{P}{\alpha + (m + \gamma)/I} \quad (9.12)$$

Therefore for P=16 K and $\alpha = 21$, the processing power η' varies between 780.2 MOPS when $(m + \gamma)/I \ll 0.1$ and 712.34 MOPS when $(m + \gamma)/I$ is

9.3. Highly Balanced Computations

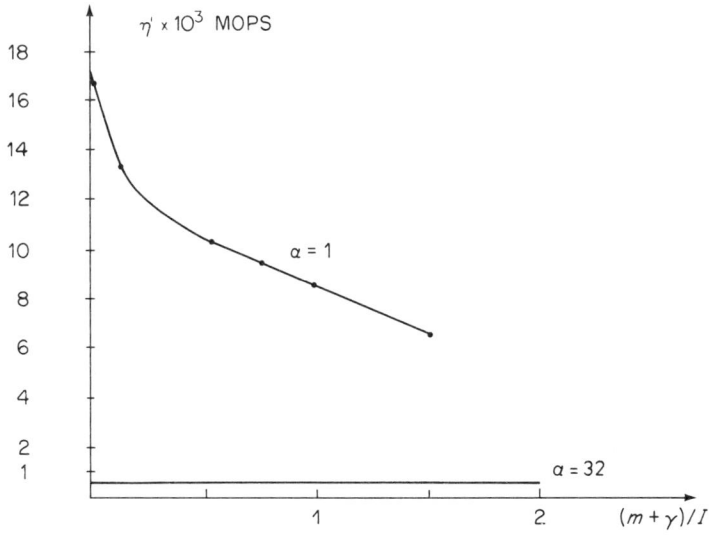

Figure 9.4: η' processing power in MOPS of the Connection Machine without ROUTER network access

equal to 2. We see that though this peak performance is sensitive to local communications, the effect is relatively moderate.

In Fig. 9.4 we plot η' against $(m+\gamma)/I$ for $\alpha = 21$.

Let us now consider the effect of the RN. To do so we take the ratio η/η' to examine the reduction in performance due to the RN:

$$\frac{\eta}{\eta'} = \left[1 + \frac{0.583\Pi f_r}{\alpha I + m + \gamma}\right]^{-1} \qquad (9.13)$$

The above relation allows us to correct the curves given in Fig. 9.4 in order to take into account the slow-down introduced by the RN.

On Fig. 9.5 we plot η/η' as a percentage, for $I = 1$, $I = 10$ and $I = 100$ instructions, $\alpha = 21$, as well as for $\alpha = 1$ and $\alpha = 0.1$, against Πf_r which varies from 0 to 12 (its largest possible value when $\Pi=12$ and $f_r=1$).

These two last values of α are of no practical interest today, but serve to indicate the degradation of the RN on a hypothetical future very fast CM.

We see that for $\alpha = 21$, which corresponds to the 21 microsecond instruction execution time, the RN has no practical effect on performance degradation since η'/η is reduced at most by 3 percent if I is larger than ten instructions. The degradation only becomes significant for a small value of I if we had a much faster machine with 1 microsecond ($\alpha = 1$) instruction

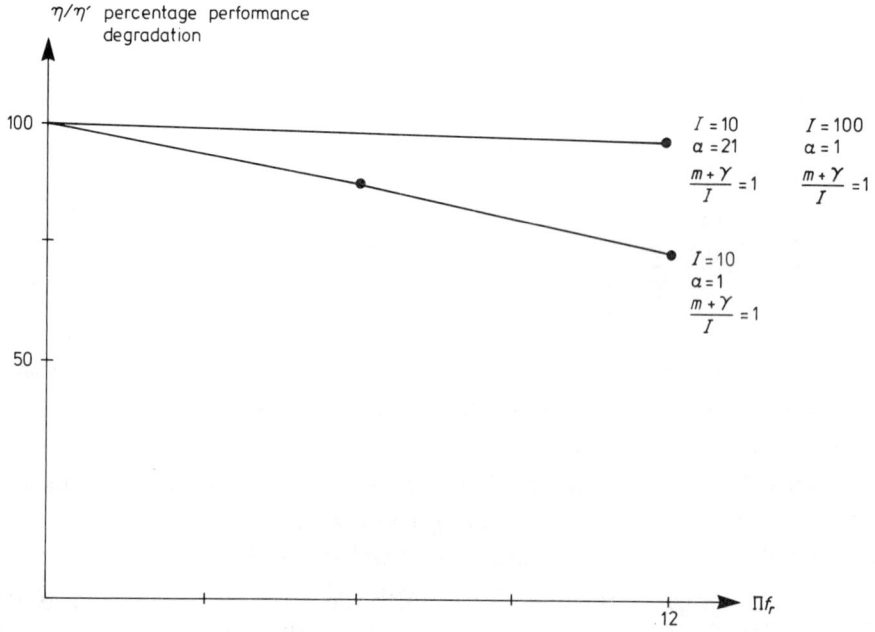

Figure 9.5: Percentage reduction in processing power of the CM due to the RN slow-down without queueing at the ROUTER

execution times.

9.3.2 A simple concrete example

Consider the computation graph shown on Fig. 9.3. Each individual task, executed on processor i at some time t, takes the form:

begin repeat indefinitely
wait for messages **from** $i - 1$ **and** $i + 1$;
    receive messages
    $g_i(t) \leftarrow G[g_{i-1}(t),$ messages$]$;
    send messages **to** $i - 1$ **and** $i + 1$;
end.

Here G is the function computed by each of the processors at each step. With respect to the discussion of the previous section, the following times can be associated with this code. The **wait for** instruction takes time M. The code beginning with **receive** and including the assignment $g_i(t) \leftarrow G[.]$, will execute I instructions taking (on the average) αI time units. The **send** instruction will take time m, including the time necessary for processing all message sending but excluding the principal transmission time; indeed, we assume that all messages sent are guaranteed to arrive so that a processor does not need to wait to be informed that a message it has sent has effectively arrived. From Fig. 9.3 we have $f_N = 0.75$, $f_r = 0.0625$ and $L = 2$ Taking unit time to be $T = 1$ microsecond, $\gamma = 1$, and $\alpha = 21$ (so that we have a 21 microsecond instruction execution time), $I = 100$, $m = 1$, we see that Λf_r is very small so that

$$M \cong 1 + 0.0364\Pi$$

For this application with some care it should be easy to implement the application so as to obtain $\Pi = 1.5$; indeed for each message entering the RN, it seems possible to address it either to a ROUTER at a single hop distance or a two hop distance. We then have $M \approx 1.05$. From (11) we have $\eta \approx 761.1$ MOPS for a 16 K processor CM.

9.4 Conclusions

In this chapter we have considered the performance of the Connection Machine architecture. Special emphasis has been placed on the performance degradation which may be expected due to communication delays between processors. Hence special attention has been placed on the architecture of the Connection Machine communication network including the NEWS and ROUTER networks. In particular, the TDMA protocol of the ROUTER Network has been modelled using a queueing model with vacation times. Both local communication, among processors connected to the same NEWS network, and remote communication via the ROUTER network has been considered. This has lead us to present a quantitative characterization of the concept of "local sphere of computation" introduced for the CM in [16].

The communication delay between processors has been computed from a queueing model and introduced into the model of the global architecture. This has yielded a formula for the performance degradation of the CM processing power as a function of communication locality and as a function of parameters of the architecture. A simple example of a SIMD computation has been provided in order to illustrate the methodlogy we have have developed.

Our example shows that with some care, and assuming parameters currently announced for the CM, this degradation can be quite small as long as the number of arithmetic operations I executed between successive communication steps exceeds 10. For lower values of I the degradation can become quite significant important.

9.5 Bibliography

In this chapter we have considered the performance of the Connection Machine architecture. Special emphasis has been placed on the performance degradation which may be expected from the communication between processors. Both local communication, among processors connected to the same NEWS network, and remote communication via the ROUTER network has been considered. Figures for this performance degradation have been obtained using simple analytical models. Our results show that with some care this degradation becomes negligible for the CM as long as the number of arithmetic operations I executed between successive communication steps exceeds 10. For lower values of I the degradation can become important.

The results in this chapter are essentially original. The references given below provide further reading on the CM and on its usage and performance with various applications.

[1] Hillis, W.D., 'The Connection Machine', MIT Press, Cambridge, Mass.,

9.4. Bibliography

USA (1985).

[2] Hillis, W.D., 'The Connection Machine: A Computer Architecture Based on Cellular Automata', *Physica*, Vol. 10, pp. 213–228, (1984).

[3] Frenkel, K.A., 'Evaluating Two Massively Parallel Machines', *Communications of the ACM*, Vol. 29, No. 8 (August 1986).

[4] Batcher, K.E., 'Architecture of a Massively Parallel Processor', *Proceedings of the 7th Annual Int. Symp. on Computer Architecture*, La Baule, France (May 1980).

[5] BBN Laboratories, 'Butterfly Parallel Processor Overview', *BBN*, Cambridge, Massachusetts, USA (December 1985).

[6] Intel Corporation, *iPSC System Overview* (October 1985).

[7] Flanders, P.M., Hunt S.F., Reddaway, S.F. and Parkinson D., 'Efficient High Speed Computing with the Distributed Array Processor', *Proceedings of the Symp. on High Speed Computer and Algorithm Organization*, University of Illinois, USA, Academic Press (1977).

[8] 'Connection Machine Model CM-2 Technical Summary', *Thinking Machines Technical Report HA87-4*, Thinking Machines Corporation, Cambridge, Mass., USA (April 1987).

[9] Broomell, G. and Heath, J.R., 'Classification Categories and Historical Development of Circuit Switching Topologies', *Computing Surveys*, Vol. 15 (June 1983).

[10] Levitan, S.P., 'Measuring Communication Structures in Parallel Architectures and Algorithms', in *The Characteristics of Parallel Algorithms*, pp. 101–137, Jamieson, L.H., Gannon, D.B. and Douglas, R.J. (eds), MIT Press, Cambridge, Mass., USA (1987).

[11] Little, J.J., 'Parallel algorithms for Computer Vision on the Connection Machine', *AI Memo 928*, Massachusetts Institute of Technology, Artificial Intelligence Laboratory, Cambridge, Massachusetts, USA (November 1986).

[12] Flynn, A.M. and Harris, J.G., 'Recognition Algorithms for the Connection Machine', *Proceedings of the 9th Int. Joint Conf. on Artificial Intelligence*, Los Angeles, USA, pp. 57–60 (August 1985).

[13] Harris, J.G. and Flynn, A.M., 'Object Recognition Using the Connection Machine's Router', *Proceedings IEEE 1986 Conf. Computer Vision and Pattern Recognition*, pp. 134–139 (May 1986).

[14] Stanfill, C. and Kahle, B., 'Parallel Free Text Search on the Connection Machine System', *Communications of the ACM*, Vol. 29, No. 12 (December 1986).

[15] Stanfill, C. and Waltz, D., 'Toward Memory-based Reasoning', *Communications of the ACM*, Vol. 29, No. 12 (December 1986).

[16] Upton, R.A. and Tripathi, S.K., 'On the Performance Evaluation of Fine-Grained SIMD Computer Architectures: an Analysis of the Connection Machine', *High Performance Computer Systems*, Gelenbe,E. (ed.), Elsevier Science Publishers, North-Holland, Amsterdam (1988).

[17] Gelenbe, E. and Mitrani, I., *Analysis and Synthesis of Computer Systems*, Academic Press, London and New York (1980).

[18] Gelenbe, E. and Iasnogorodsky, R. 'A Queue with Server of Walking Type', *Annales de l'Institut Henri Poincaré, Série B (Probabilité et Statistiques)*, Vol. XVI, No. 1, pp. 63–73 (1980).

Index

Activity Set Model 22, 25–6, 30
acyclic random graphs as models of
    parallel programs 67–91
  asymptotic analysis of the mean
      processing time 76–8
  asymptotic properties of the
      speed-up 75–6
  bibliography 90–1
  comparison of the approximation
      with simulation results 78–9
  estimation of the probability of
      precedence between tasks 79–83
  random graph model for a family of
      programs 72–4
  task graphs with communication
      times between tasks 83–90
ALU (arithmetic and logical unit) and
    the Connection Machine 140
Amdahl's law and multiprocessor
    speed-up 21–31
  amendment to Amdahl's law 23–5
  bibliography 30–1
  communication time between
      parallel processors 24–5
  model of intrinsic program behaviour
      25–9
architectures
  Connection Machine 137–52
  distributed 1–2, 9–12
  Hypercube 2, 10, 15–17, 25
  logic-in-memory 137
  multiprocessor and distributed
      systems compared 1–2
  parallel 7–20, 49–65; see also
      parallel programs
  simple array or vector processor
      123–5
  supercomputers 121–36

array processors
  defined 8–9
  performance potential and
      limitations 10–11
  simplest supercomputer 123–5
  supercomputer with n scalar
      processors and m vector
      processors 125–8
  supercomputers with limited number
      of vector processors 128–32
artificial intelligence 137

bandwidth of networks 36–42
Baseline networks 33–48
Batson, Alan 22n
benchmarks (BMK) 132–4
bibliography
  acyclic random graphs as models of
      parallel programs 90–1
  Connection Machine 152–4
  interconnection networks 46–8
  multiprocessor architecture, program
      structure and machine
      performance 19–20
  multiprocessor performance with
      task-graph models 117–19
  multiprocessor speed-up and
      Amdahl's law 30–1
  parallel program performance: series-
      parallel program structures 64–5
  supercomputer performance
      evaluation 134–5
BMK (benchmark) characteristics 132–4
bus or interconnection network
  of array processor 9
  and performance 12–14
  see also interconnection networks

155

cache memory 13−15
CDC 7600 122
CDC CYBER 205 and 30 124−5, 127
CM see Connection Machine
coarse-grained parallelism 8, 9
COMM (communication system) 12
communication times
  between tasks in task graphs 68, 83−90
  in ROUTER networks 140−2
Connection Machine (CM) 17, 121, 137−54
  bibliography 152−4
  highly balanced computations 146−51
  ROUTER Network performance 141−6, 148−51
CRAY-1 124−5
critical path in a task graph 69−72

data flow architectures 9
date of first supercomputer 122
Denning, Peter 22n
distributed architectures
  defined 9
  performance potential and limitations 10−12
DROP network model 35−42

ETA GF30 121−2
execution time
  for SPTG 58−64
  for task graphs 69−90

fine-grained parallelism 8, 9
Flip networks 33

GIGAFLOPS definition 121
  examples of 122, 124, 128
granularity 8−11

heat equation, solution of 147−51
history of multiprocessors 1−2, 122
HOLD network model 35−6, 42−6
HOST 16
Hypercube architecture 2, 10, 15−17, 25

IBM 3090 121
indegree 80
Indirect Binary Cube networks 33
infinite tree 59
interconnection networks 33−48
  bandwidth of the Baseline and Omega Networks with the DROP approach 36−40
  bandwidth of the DROP model 41−2
  bibliography 46−8
  bus or switch 12−14
  numerical solution of the DROP model 40−1
  of array processor 9
  the HOLD network model 42−6

job response time in a task graph 98−103

Lattice Gas Machine 18−19
logic-in-memory architecture 137
Los Alamos benchmark characteristics 132−4

main memory banks 12−15
make-span 74
mean processing time in task graphs, asymptotic analysis of 76−8
measures of performance, Time (T), Cost (C), Throughput (θ) and Reliability/Reconfigurability 10−11
message time matrix 84
MFLOPS definition 124
MIMD (multiple instruction multiple data) 9, 16
multiprocessor architecture, program structure, and machine performance 7−20
  bibliography 19−20
  different types of multiprocessor 15−19
  performance issues in some typical multiprocessor architectures 12−15
  performance potential and limitations of parallel computer architectures 10−12
multiprocessor performance with task-graph models 93−119
  analysis of multiprocessor systems with different types of parallel programs 107−9
  bibliography 117−19
  derivation of the job response time 98−103
  numerical examples and model validation 103−7
  the case of systems with processors of different types 109−17

Index

the multiprocessor system model,
  general and simplified 94–8
multiprocessor speed-up and Amdahl's
  law 21–31

nano-instructions 140
Navier-Stokes equations 18
networks *see* interconnection networks
  and names of networks
NEWS (North-East-West-South)
  network and the Connection
  Machine 17, 138–52

Omega networks 33, 36–40
operating system and performance
  limitations 14–15

parallel architectures 7–20, 49–65;
  see also parallel programs
parallel computer architecture (PCA)
  7–12
  four classes
    array processors 8–9
    data flow architectures 9–10
    distributed architectures 9
    multiprocessors 9
  performance potential and
    limitations 10–12
parallel program performance: series-
  parallel program structures 49–65
  bibliography 64–5
  distribution of program execution or
    completion time 58–9
  numerical solution for the execution
    time distribution function 60–4
  the SPTG model of program
    structure 50–8
parallel programs
  acyclic random graphs as models of
    67–91
  multiprocessor systems with different
    types of 107–9
parallel system architecture (PSA) 7–8
path in task graphs 69–72
PCA (parallel computer architecture)
  7–12
petit cycle 139
Poisson process for the arrival of jobs
  93, 94, 97–103, 108–12, 143–5
potentially parallel application (PPA)
  7–9
power, processing 121–8

PPA (potentially parallel application)
  7–9
precedence
  matrix 84
  probability of, between tasks in task
    graphs 79–83
Process Working Set Model 22n
processing power 121–8
PSA (parallel system architecture) 7–8

queueing
  and the performance of the ROUTER
    Network 141–6
  in multiprocessor performance with
    task-graph models 93–117

R-R (register to register) scheme 125
random graphs *see* acyclic random
  graphs
response time of a job 98–103
ROUTER Network (RN) and the
  Connection Machine 138–52

scalar processors 125–32
series-parallel task graphs *see* SPTG
SIMD (single instruction multiple data)
  8, 16, 17, 140
simulations for task graphs 78–9,
  88–90, 103–7
slot traffic 145
speed of electronic components,
  limitations of 2
speed-up
  and Amdahl's law 21–31
  asymptotic properties of, in task
    graphs 74–6
  estimating probability of precedence
    for determining, in task graphs
    79–83
  simulation of asymptotic, with
    communication times in task
    graphs 88–90
SPTG (series-parallel task graphs)
  50–8
  in multiple processor system 115–17
  model of program structure 50–2
  statistical properties of the family of
    55–8
  stochastic model for family of 52–5
supercomputer performance evaluation
  121–35
  bibliography 134–5
  date of appearance 122

supercomputer performance evaluation (*cont.*)
   Los Alamos benchmark characteristics 132–4
   performance of a single processor 123–5
   supercomputers with a limited number of vector processing facilities 128–32
   supercomputers with multiple vector processors 125–8

task graphs *see* acyclic random graphs; multiprocessor performance with task-graph models; SPTG
task, definition 50–1
TDMA (Time-Division-Multiple-Access) and the Connection Machine 17, 139, 152
TERAFLOP-1 121
Thinking Machines Corporation 17, 121, 137n

vector processors *see* array processors